Steelhead Fly Fishing Nez Perce Country

Snake River Tributaries

RIVERS · ANGLERS · FLIES · ORIGINS

Dan Landeen

Grande Ronde River at Shumaker Grade.

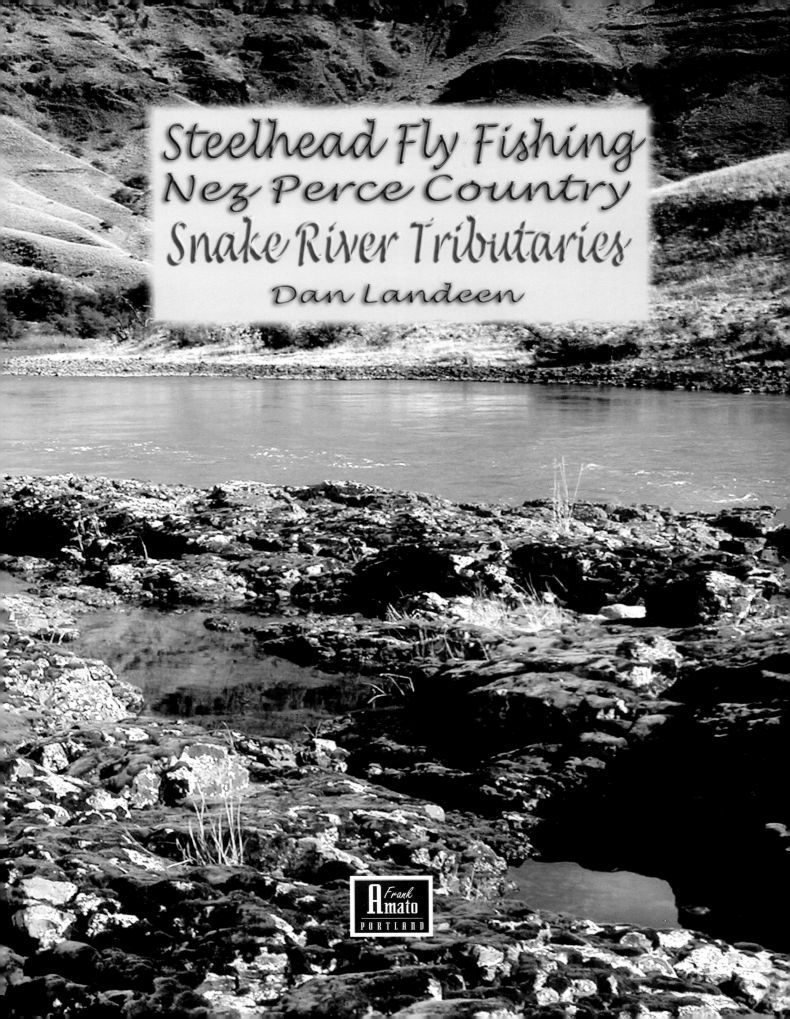

Steelhead Fly Fishing
Nez Perce Country
Snake River Tributaries

Dan Landeen

Frank Amato
PORTLAND

Dedication

To my father for ensuring that all his sons learned how to fish for brook trout in Wyoming and to my grandfather Ezra Harding who gave me my first fly fishing lessons on trout streams near Anaconda, Montana. This book is also dedicated to those fly fishermen that were interviewed for the book that have since passed away including Paul Nolt, Jim Green, Dave Engebretson, and Bob Black. I would also like to dedicate this book to the many anglers that were interviewed but due to publishing constraints did not have a major chapter in the book. These include Jack Rogers, Jay Hessee, Perk Lyda, Jim Palmershein, Dale Knoche, Mark Lamb, Jerry Cebula, Glen Brackett, Bill McMillan, Levi Carson, Jim Adams, and Bill McAffee (journal).

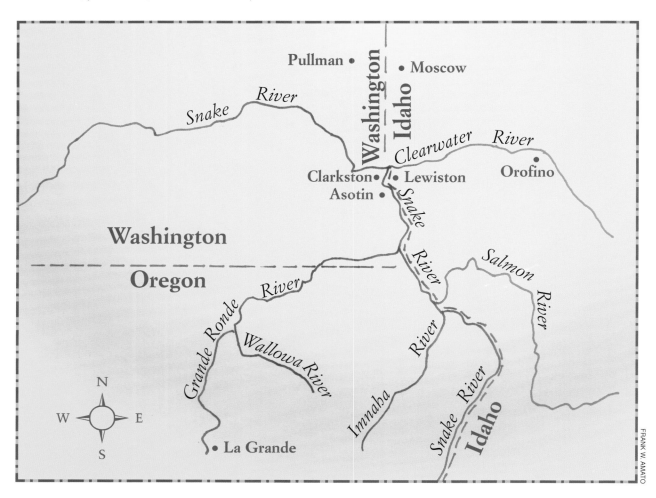

FRANK W. AMATO

All inquiries should be addressed to:

Frank Amato Publications, Inc, P.O. Box 82112, Portland, Oregon 97282

503•653•8108 • www.amatobooks.com

Angler profile photographs were provided by the angler, family members or friends, Dan Callahan provided photographs for the Callahan Gallery, all other photographs by the author unless otherwise noted.

Book & Cover Design: Kathy Johnson
Printed in Hong Kong
Softbound ISBN: 1-57188-383-5   UPC: 0-81127-00217-7
Hardbound ISBN: 1-57188-384-3   UPC: 0-81127-00218-4
Limited Edition ISBN: 1-57188-385-1   UPC: 0-81127-00219-1

1 3 5 7 9 10 8 6 4 2

Asotin Creek Canyon.

CONTENTS

Preface

This is not a "where to go" book. Fly-fishing as much as anything is about discovery. This book will only point one in the general direction. It profiles fly-fishermen, provides historical information, and philosophies and techniques that have proven successful over time. Stories and experiences from both young and old are included. Many of the anglers tie and use traditional flies with some local variation, while others have developed original patterns.

The original intent was to interview and profile anglers living in the Lewiston area and as far north as Moscow/Pullman and south to Joseph, Oregon. However, Jim Green was quick to point out that the book would not be complete if we didn't include anglers who have fished these waters for over 30 years yet reside elsewhere.

The Nez Perce Indians, who have always relied on the area's rivers for spiritual and physical sustenance, will tell you that all things are related, that all things are connected and that all of us including plants and animals are part of one great circle. What I discovered is that all fly-fishermen are related and are also part of one big circle.

Anglers like Jimmy Green, Rick Miller, Bill Nelson, Walter Price, Bob Weddell, Keith Stonebraker, Duke Parkening, Craig Lannigan, LeRoy Hyatt and others who have a lot of experience were acquainted with many of the early fly-fishing pioneers. They took instruction from such anglers as Wes Drain, Enos Bradner, Walter Powell, Ralph Wahl, Walter Johnson, Ted Trueblood, and Bill Schaadt. They fished with them, or were influenced by others who knew them or by something they happened to scribble down on paper. These men in turn have passed their knowledge to the next generation. Those who pursue steelhead with a fly have common ancestry.

Originally, I thought the emphasis would be on technique and pattern but the people I interviewed who are passionate about fly-fishing and steelhead and salmon helped me realize the larger issue. As Duke Parkening pointed out, "rods, reels, techniques and patterns are meaningless without the resource."

We all need to look at the larger picture and do what we can as individuals and a society to ensure that anadromous fish will not disappear from the Pacific Northwest and elsewhere.

More than anything I have come to realize that as a society we need to get serious about saving and restoring salmon and steelhead. We shouldn't just rely on a few dedicated folks like the Truebloods, Stonebrakers, Engerbretsons and Pettits of the world to fight the battle. Our anadromous species are precious resources. One of the things that defines the health and integrity of rivers like the Columbia, Snake, Clearwater, and Grande Ronde is the existence of these species. How we treat our rivers tells us a lot about ourselves.

Nez Perce tribal member Jaime Pinkham says that we need to "view the salmon and steelhead as the miner's canaries. We flippantly seem to be willing to discard one resource, then another, and another. Where does it all end?"

Leopold said, "The outstanding scientific discovery of the twentieth century is not television, or radio, but rather the com-

Asotin Creek is a tributary of the Snake River.

plexity of the land organism. Only those who know the most about it can appreciate how little we know about it. The last word in ignorance is the man who says of an animal or plant: "What good is it?" If the land mechanism as a whole is good, then every part is good, whether we understand it or not. If the biota, in the course of eons, has built something we like but do not understand, then who but a fool would discard seemingly useless parts? To keep every cog and wheel is the first precaution of intelligent tinkering."

If we can't marshal the support and resources to save these magnificent creatures we are not nearly as smart as we think we are. Technology can be a wonderful thing, but feeling the pull of a steelhead as it inhales your Green Butt Skunk on the swing is not such a bad thing either.

The majority of the anglers that are included in this book were interviewed from the fall of 2001 to the spring of 2002 and the write-ups of each angler represent what they actually said. I did make minor editorial changes in some cases to ensure clarity and grammatical accuracy.

I would like to acknowledge the cooperation of the many anglers who I was able to interview and include in this book. A special thanks to Jim Hepworth former editor of Confluence Press and fishing partner who had the original idea for this book.

Chronology

12–16 Million Years Ago: The Columbia River Basalts are formed, which in turn form the canyons and valleys of the Snake River system.

1–2 Million Years Ago: Idaho Lake overflows near Oxbow thus creating the Snake River's present course between Oregon and Idaho and eventually into the Columbia River drainage.

15,000 Years Ago: Lake Bonneville overflows at Red Rock Pass releasing a large volume of water into the Snake River.

10,000 Years Ago: As a result of the Missoula Flood water is backed up into the Clearwater Valley to a depth of 500-600 feet.

8,000–10,000 Years Ago: First evidence of human occupation along the Clearwater, Snake, and Grande Ronde rivers. Steelhead, salmon, and other species were harvested each year. Pacific lampreys were also common to all of the rivers and were also harvested in large numbers each year. Evidence suggests that the people were catching salmon and steelhead with bone hooks and grouse feathers for the past 200 years.

6,000 Years Ago: Mt. Mazama, Crater Lake, exploded about 6,600 years ago, well into the period of exploration and settlement by Native Americans. A layer of Mt. Mazama ash is well represented throughout the area.

1920s

1927 Inland Power Company constructs the Clearwater or Lewiston Dam three miles upstream from the mouth of the Clearwater River. This dam had the effect of eliminating the coho run and also had devastating effects on chinook, steelhead, and Pacific lampreys.

1930s

1933 Construction of the Bonneville Dam on the Columbia River begins

1938 Paul Nolt, Don Shook, and Norm Lawrence from Lewiston fly-fish the Grande Ronde for steelhead at Shumaker Grade for the first time.

1940s

1940 Roads to mouth of Grande Ronde from Asotin and Rattlesnake Grade to Bogan's Oasis are constructed.

1943 Nuclear reactors that produce weapons-grade plutonium used in the bombs that effectively end World War II are built as part of the Manhattan Project at Hanford along the Columbia River in eastern Washington.

1945 Rick Miller from Everett, Washington is one of the first outsiders to catch steelhead on a fly on the Grande Ronde.

1945 John Carsow, a medical doctor from Lewiston, starts fly-fishing the Grande Ronde.

1948 Bill Nelson, a student at the University of Idaho, fly-fishes the Grande Ronde for the first time and succeeds in just catching smallmouth bass.

1950s

1951 Nez Perce tribal member Elmer Crow, Sr. catches a steelhead on a fly on the Clearwater River near Orofino, Idaho.

1951 Bob and Beverly Black fish the Grande Ronde for the first time at Bogan's Oasis.

1955 Bill Nelson's group from Everett, Washington which includes Rick Miller, Lew Bell and Dick Denman fish the Grande Ronde for the first time.

1955 Paul Ramlow is introduced to the Grande Ronde by his friend Rick Miller and has fished it every year since then with his two-handed bamboo rods.

1955 Fishermen such as Benton Collins and Clark Hamilton from the Palouse start fishing the Grande Ronde. Benton has his photo taken with a Grande Ronde fish by Rex Gerlach that shows up in a *Field & Stream* article in 1966.

1957 Young 17-year-old Jake Gulke is befriended by Bill Nelson's group and has fly-fished the Grande Ronde ever since.

1957 The completion of the Dalles Dam on the Columbia destroys Celilo Falls which was the main gathering and fishing place for salmon for thousands of years for all the Columbia Basin Tribes.

1958 Elmer Crow Jr., a Nez Perce Indian, catches a steelhead on a bee pattern in Kelly Creek and is one of the few who have ever caught steelhead on a fly in the North Fork drainage.

1958 Fenton Roskelly, an outdoor writer for the Spokane newspapers, starts fly-fishing the Ronde and over the years writes several newspaper articles about the local rivers.

1957-59 Wes Drain starts fishing the Grande Ronde with Bill Nelson's group and in the early 70s almost loses his life in a boating accident on the Snake River below Heller's Bar.

1950s Thorson Bennett born in Elgin, Oregon may have started fly-fishing the Grande Ronde in the late 50s. He is known for his "Chappie" fly.

1960s

1960 Ted Trueblood fishes the Grande Ronde for the first time.

1961 Ice Harbor Dam becomes the first dam to be built on the Snake River.

1961 Ted Trueblood writes the first steelhead fly-fishing article about the Grande Ronde in *True Magazine* but refers to it as the "unnamed river."

1962 Ken Anderson and Ed Ward from the Walt Disney Studios in California fish the Clearwater with Ted Trueblood.

1962 Jack Rogers from Pullman starts fishing the Grande Ronde with his friends and is mentored by Benton Collins and later on Keith Stonebraker.

1962 Congress authorizes the Army Corp of Engineers to construct a dam at Asotin, Washington.

1963 Perk Lyda from Orofino becomes the first licensed fishing guide on the Clearwater.

1963 Duke Parkening, Milt Kahl, Ken Petersen, and Mel Leven from California and the Disney studios start fishing the local rivers.

1963 The Fly-fishing Federation is formed by Bill Nelson and his friends in Eugene, Oregon. The idea for the federation came out of discussions on the Grande Ronde River when Bill and his friends would fish every October. Noted anglers like Jimmy Green, Ted Trueblood, and Lee Wulff were keynote speakers.

1964 Walt (Dub) Price introduces grease lining on the Grande Ronde. He writes about this technique in "The Creel" in 1966.

1965 Bob Weddell moves from California to Boise, Idaho and starts fishing on the Salmon River.

1965 Tom Morgan and Keith Stonebraker first start fishing for steelhead with a fly on the Clearwater and Grande Ronde.

1966 Rex Gerlach writes an article about steelhead fly-fishing in *Field & Stream* Magazine and names the Ronde for the first time.

1966 Jim and Carol Green fish the Grande Ronde for the first time with Ted Trueblood

1966 Bob Weddell moves to Orofino from Boise and starts catching steelhead on the Clearwater. He learns how to grease line from Walt Price on the Grande Ronde in 1967 and becomes the first one to grease line on the Clearwater where he in turn introduces the technique to Keith Stonebraker, Duke Parkening, Tom Morgan, and Glen Brackett.

1966 Local resident Keith Stonebraker catches his first steelhead on a fly (Fall Favorite) on the Clearwater and is one of the first to use Bombers on the Clearwater.

1967 Ted Trueblood writes an article in Field & Stream about the negative impacts of dams on the Columbia and Snake rivers.

1967 Tom Morgan moves to Clarkston, Washington and fishes with Bob Weddell, Keith Stonebraker, and Glen Brackett. Tom goes on to own the Winston Rod Company with Glen Brackett and later on forms his own company of Morgan Rodsmiths where he invents a new hand mill for bamboo rod makers.

1967 Glen Brackett starts fishing the Clearwater with Bob Weddell and is one of the first to use a riffle hitch almost exclusively. Glen teams with Tom Morgan in 1985 to run the Winston Rod Company.

1967 Famous fishermen such as Ted Trueblood and Lee Wulff make the first fly-fishing steelhead television productions on the Grande Ronde..

1968 Salmon smolt are barged for the first time.

1969 Lower Monumental Dam is completed and comes on line.

1969 Duke Parkening completes the building of his new home on the Middle Fork of the Clearwater.

1970s

1970 Gale House from Walla Walla and friend of Tom Morgan and Keith Stonebraker starts fishing the Clearwater.

1970 Little Goose Dam on the Snake River is completed.

1970 Several organizations file suit to halt construction of Lower Granite Dam.

1970 Wes Drain almost drowns in boating accident in the Snake River below Heller's Bar.

1970 In March the Association of Northwest Steelheaders files suit against the Corp to halt construction of Lower Granite Dam and to deauthorize the dam at Asotin.

1971 Glen Brackett introduces Bill McAffee to the area in 1971. Bill fished for 20 years until his untimely death 1991.

1971 Steve Pettit moves to the area and is hired by the State of Idaho as a fisheries biologist. He soon develops a reputation as a first-rate steelheader and his knowledge of the biology and associated politics of steelhead are second to none.

1972 Craig Lannigan and LeRoy Hyatt, both Lewiston residents, start fly-fishing for steelhead. Craig is one of the premier steelheaders in the area and LeRoy becomes a professional fly tier and teams with Dave Engerbretson eventually to host a fly-tying television show on PBS

1972 Dave Engerbretson moves to Moscow, ID from Pennsylvania where he learned to fly-fish from George Harvey. Dave writes many articles for outdoor magazines and, largely due to his efforts, convinces the Department of the Interior not to log the Kelly Creek watershed in the 1990s.

1973 The Clearwater Dam or Lewiston Dam is taken out.

1973 Partly due to previous efforts of attorney and longtime steelhead fly-fisherman Lew Bell the lower Grande Ronde becomes a catch-and-release section.

1973 Bill Alspach, who grew up in Lewiston and fished all his life, learns how to fly-fish and becomes one of the better local fly-fishers the area has ever produced. Bill is responsible for the local steelhead pattern know as the "Beats Me."

1974 Meetings are held in Clarkston, WA regarding catch-and-release regulations for the Grande Ronde.

1975 The Grande Ronde is closed to fishing but the area from the confluence to the county bridge is opened to the new catch-and-release regulations.

1975 Lower Granite Dam which is the last dam to be built on the Snake River is completed and slack water reaches Lewiston, Idaho.

1977 Steve Pettit conducts landmark catch-and-release study.

1978 Dworshak Dam on the North Fork River is completed

1978 Jeff Jarrett from Orofino starts guiding on the Clearwater.

1970s Jack Hemmingway builds a home above the Grande Ronde and serves on the Idaho Fish and Game Commission with Keith Stonebraker.

1980s

1980 Jimmy Green builds the first prototype two-handed graphite rod.

1985 Mac Huff from Enterprise, Oregon begins guiding on the Grande Ronde.

1982 Gordie Olsen learns how to fly-fish from his friend Jake Gulke and works with Jimmy Green on fly line and rod design.

1985 Jim Vincent writes an article about riffle hitching on the Clearwater and interviews Bob Weddell and Glen Brackett.

1988 President Reagan signs a bill that effectively prohibits the licensing of more dams on the Snake River and the Asotin Dam Project is halted for good.

1988 Jim and Carol Green build a home above the lower Grande Ronde

1990s

1991 Terry Nab, long-time Atlantic salmon fly-fisherman, moves to Lewiston and is one of the area's premier steelhead fly-fishermen.

1991 Long-time Clearwater River fly-fisherman Bill McAfee dies in bush plane accident in Alaska.

1992 Dale Knoche friend and fishing partner of Jim Green builds a home next to the Grande Ronde.

1995 Dave Clark retires and moves to Clarkston so he can steelhead fish.

1997 John Toker moves from Pennsylvania to Pullman and within a short amount of time has become recognized as one of the better fly-fishermen. John is mentored by Dave Engerbretson, Stan Hendrickson, Al Burr, and Craig Lannigan.

1998 Steelhead are placed on the Endangered Species List.

2000s

2001 One of the largest steelhead runs ever recorded draws record numbers of anglers.

2002 Environmental Protection Agency releases a report that documents contamination in fish in the Columbia River.

Pine tree next to the Grande Ronde River.

North Fork of the Clearwater River in the fall.

Nez Perce Country

The Northern Rockies stretch from Yellowstone National Park in northwest Wyoming north through western Montana, north and central Idaho and northeastern Washington to the Canadian border. They include Idaho's Clearwater and Salmon River mountains, along with the Bitterroot Range along the Idaho-Montana border.

They were formed by varied geological processes that date back to the Triassic Period, 230 million years ago. Within the last 25 million years, during the Miocene Epoch, a number of volcanic episodes arising at the western edge of the Northern Rockies produced huge volumes of basalt lava. This lava covered much of the Columbia Plateau. The last of these episodes occurred primarily between 16 and 12 millions years ago, and these flows are collectively known as the Columbia River Basalt. They form most of the columns and flows seen on the canyon walls along the lower Snake and Clearwater canyons. Basalt from these eruptions oozed up through fractures and fissures in the ground, and many of them flowed in great volumes through the Columbia River Gorge all the way to the Pacific Ocean.

Between some of the lava flows there were long periods of inactivity in which weathered surfaces developed. Soils and sediments washed from these surfaces and were deposited in lakes, streambeds, or depressions throughout the basaltic plains. Later, lava flows erupted over the same areas and covered these slopes and sedimentary deposits, forming a cap over layers of sand, gravel, silt, and sometimes volcanic ash. Some of these sedimentary interbeds are exposed on canyon walls below the elevation of the present plateaus. Some of the deposits of sand, gravel, and clay in these interbeds are of economic value.

The deep canyons, gorges, and river valleys that are now home to the Snake, Salmon, Imnaha, and Grande Ronde rivers were formed primarily during and after the eruption of the Columbia River Basalts. Geologists can see where younger eruptions at times filled in areas of canyons, requiring the rivers to find alternate routes or to cut through the new flows. During the Miocene Epoch, when the Columbia River Basalts were being erupted, geologic mountain-building forces were lifting the eastern edge of the province, which encouraged the rivers to cut ever more deeply as the watersheds developed their westward drainages.

Most geologists agree that the present course of the Snake River is a very late development in geological terms. In late Pleistocene times, 1-2 million years ago, the river probably followed a course from east to west through Idaho. Idaho Lake, that was formed in pre Pleistocene times, spilled over near Oxbow and started flowing northward thus creating its present course between Oregon and Idaho and eventually into the Columbia River drainage. When Idaho Lake spilled over it found a new outlet into the headwaters of a northward-flowing Salmon River tributary. Thus, the new course of the Snake River for the first time into the Columbia drainage was initiated (Wheeler and Cook, 1954).

According to Vallier (1998), the Snake River as we now know it began flowing directly into the Columbia River about 2-6 million years ago. Vallier indicates that if we were to step back in time 50,000-100,000 years we would see very little change in the Snake River. We would still recognize the same tributary streams and even some of the same gravel bars.

Lupher and Warren (1942) think that the early Pleistocene Snake "was a small stream in comparison to the present Snake River, perhaps less than 100 feet wide in some places. It carries gravels that are much finer than the coarse cobble gravels of the modern Snake."

One of the next major occurrences to impact the Snake River was the Bonneville Flood. During the Pleistocene there were a number of inland ice age lakes of considerable size. One of these was Lake Bonneville and the only surviving remnant of that lake is the Great Salt Lake in Utah. About 15,000 years ago Lake Bonneville reached its greatest height and flowed over Red Rock Pass and discharged a great volume of water down the Snake River in southern Idaho. Scientists have indicated that parts of the Snake River Canyon were flooded to a depth of 400 feet. Today one can see abandoned channels, areas of scabland and huge boulders and gravel bars that it left in its wake.

The next major flood event that impacted this area was the final Missoula Flood episode that occurred about 12,000 years ago. Ice age glaciers had dammed the Clark's Fork River in northern Montana and southern Canada and created a lake about half the size of the present-day Lake Michigan. The dam would break and reform repeatedly, and would drain at a rate higher than any other flood ever known. Water velocity reached speeds of 45 miles per hour. By the time each flood episode had ended, water had traveled 550 miles to the Pacific Ocean and left behind a totally new landscape in its wake. The volume of water was so large that it temporarily backed up the Snake River to the Lewiston area from where the deluge struck the Snake drainage at Lyon's Ferry. At Lewiston the water is estimated to have been 600 feet deep. Huge icebergs loaded with rock debris floated in on those waters. When the ice eventually melted, boulders from as far as the Canadian Rockies, and as large as seven feet across, were left behind, strewn on the hill slopes and plains.

The Clearwater

The Clearwater drainage covers most of north central Idaho and covers 9,645 square miles. The Clearwater River originates at about 9,000 feet elevation in the Bitterroot Mountains and eventually flows into the Snake River. The main Clearwater River is 75 miles in length from its mouth to Kooskia, Idaho, where it is formed by the Middle and South Forks. The Clearwater from Orofino down is made up of the main stem or Middlefork, the North Fork and the South fork. Sixty-three miles of the main Clearwater and 11 miles of the South Fork are included in the Nez Perce Indian Reservation.

The North Fork is one of the principal tributaries of the Clearwater where it enters the river 43 miles above its mouth. It is about 135 miles long and drains some 2,440 square miles. Historically the North Fork had wonderful salmon and steelhead runs but the construction of Dworshak Dam in 1978 stopped these fish from going any further upstream. Kelly Creek, that has a reputation as a blue-ribbon cutthroat fishery, is a tributary of the North Fork.

The South Fork is about 75 miles long and contains excellent pool structures and considerable favorable spawning areas for salmonids.

The Middle Fork of the Clearwater River is about 23 miles long and is formed by the confluence of the Lochsa and Selway rivers at Lowell. From this point it flows in a westerly direction to the town of Kooskia and joins the South Fork of the Clearwater to become the main river.

Lewiston and Dworshak Dams

The Lewiston Dam was built at Lewiston three miles upstream from the mouth of the Clearwater by the Inland Power Company in 1927 and removed in 1972. It was 1,100 feet wide and at average river discharge it raised the water level to 24 feet. The large 600-acre impoundment that was formed above the dam served as a log-holding area for the Potlatch Mill.

As far as its impacts on fish went, it was devastating. According to the Regional Director of the U.S. Fish and Wildlife Service in 1954: "The construction of Lewiston Dam near the mouth of the river in 1927 seriously impeded the migration of anadromous fish and greatly reduced their abundance. Prior to the construction of that dam, the river supported large runs of salmon and steelhead trout, but due to the inadequate fish passage facilities incorporated in the structure, the salmon and Pacific lamprey runs were virtually exterminated."

The major dam on the Clearwater drainage today is Dworshak Dam constructed near the mouth of the North Fork at Orofino by the Corps of Engineers in 1978. The dam itself is within the boundaries of the Nez Perce Reservation and the lake formed by the dam extends forty miles to the northeast up the North Fork. Because of its height (700 feet) fish-passage facilities were not built and as a result the salmon and steelhead runs on the North Fork were exterminated.

The main Clearwater, South Fork and Middle Fork are managed primarily for hatchery steelhead and chinook salmon. The world's largest steelhead/salmon hatchery is located at the confluence of the North Fork and the main stem of the Clearwater near Orofino. The Clearwater is famous for the large "B-Run" steelhead that return to spawn after two to three years in the ocean. Many of these great fighters will weigh 20 pounds or more and measure 30-40 inches. Fly-fishermen from all over the United States travel to the Clearwater for the opportunity to catch one of these "B run" fish.

Starting in February, Dworshak will start releasing water which can make for difficult fly-fishing. The river runs high and off color and most of the locals quit fishing. This is about the time that the fish are finally starting to spawn and most feel that the fish deserve a rest from fishing pressure.

Many fly-fishermen on the Clearwater start fishing the catch-and-release season which goes from September through mid October. After mid October, the boat traffic or "aluminum hatch" on the river begins and many of the local fly-fishermen spend a lot less time on the Clearwater and more on the Snake.

The Snake

Today the Snake River flows south from the Yellowstone plateau past the Grand Tetons across southern Idaho into Hell's Canyon. The wild Salmon River of Idaho with its three forks joins the Snake just north of that canyon. Twenty-five miles upriver from Lewiston, the Grande Ronde empties into the Snake. At Lewiston, the Snake River turns southwest and cuts through the Columbia Basalt formation of eastern Washington, then into the Columbia River at Burbank, Washington. About one-third of the Snake River stream flow comes from the Clearwater.

The Snake River is big water and it flows uninterrupted for about 100 miles from Hell's Canyon to Lewiston. However, for all practical purposes only the last 30 miles from where the Grande Ronde enters the Snake is accessible to fly-fishermen.

Steelhead start reaching the Snake by early August. Usually at that time of year the water temperatures are hovering near the 70s which makes it very uncomfortable. Most of the fish will run up the Clearwater to escape the warm water. Later on when the temperatures drop and the fall rains arrive, they will re-enter the Snake and swim upriver to spawn in many of the smaller rivers and tributaries, including the Grande Ronde and Salmon rivers.

The Grande Ronde

The Grande Ronde is one of Oregon's most beautiful river canyons and a tributary of the famous Snake River in Hell's Canyon. This remote and deep canyon is moderately forested and surrounded by basalt cliffs. The Grande Ronde reminds many of the Deschutes, although it's much smaller. The river is relatively shallow but the dark-colored bottom is covered with large rocks that are covered with algae and are very slick.

It flows into the Snake River at Heller's Bar 25 miles from Clarkston/Lewiston. From the mouth upstream 2.5 miles to the county bridge is catch-and-release only and is one of the most popular fishing areas on the Ronde. Private homes are becoming more common in this area but so far public access to the river has remained. Other popular areas on the Ronde further upstream that have road access include Shumaker Grade accessed just outside of Anatone, WA and Bogan's Oasis located at the bottom of Rattlesnake Grade on Highway 129 that goes into Oregon. If one veers west of Bogans the road follows the river for 15-20 miles to Troy, Oregon.

Nez Perce Indians

In order to appreciate the local rivers one must realize that fishing has been an integral part of the area's history for thousands of years. Rivers are the very heart of Nez Perce country and the Snake, Clearwater, Grande Ronde, Selway, North Fork, Lochsa, Salmon, and other rivers have long provided spiritual and physical sustenance for the indigenous peoples.

Anyone who has studied the region's history will tell you that more than anything the Nez Perce were first and foremost fishermen. The Nez Perce will tell you that they have been a part of this land since time immemorial and that one of the greatest tragedies of this century is the loss of traditional fishing sites and salmon and steelhead runs throughout the Northwest.

Archeological evidence suggests that the Nez Perce have been catching steelhead and salmon and other species for at least 10,000 years and probably longer. Elizabeth Wilson, a Nez Perce woman born on the Clearwater in 1882, once observed that "salmon and steelhead were available almost year round. The steelhead came upstream from August through October and the people began catching them in November and on through the winter into February, March, and April. By June, the steelhead were gone. In July the chinook salmon began migrating and were caught in August." "So, you see," she concluded, "We could catch fish most of the year. That's the way nature provided for us."

Snake River near Asotin, Washington.

Historical Perspective

This book is not a complete history about the local rivers. It only portrays a small snapshot in time and only concentrates on a particular segment of society who derive pleasure from pursuing steelhead with a fly. River histories, like the rivers themselves, do not give up their secrets easily and what I have produced only tells part of the story.

When I started I wasn't sure where the material I gathered would lead me, but it wasn't long before I realized that my pre-conceived notions were not coming to fruition. I discovered that a history of steelhead fly-fishing on the Clearwater, Snake, and Grande Ronde rivers is in fact a microcosm of a much larger story.

From all accounts the local rivers had been fished by local bait and spinner fishermen since at least the 1930s. People in the 40s and 50s talk about the photos of B-run fish that would occasionally appear in the local newspapers, and in some cases it was that publicity that attracted fishermen from around the region.

Paul Nolt, longtime area resident, said that fishing wasn't that big of a deal in those early years. People didn't have much leisure time to spend fishing and transportation was a problem. Paul said if you did much fishing you were frowned on by society and considered lazy. He also said that in those days it was legal to spear and snag steelhead and salmon and many of the locals would catch the fish using those methods.

Paul, who was the owner and founder of Lolo Sporting Goods in 1955 in Lewiston, said that fly-fishing for steelhead didn't really get popular until anglers like Ted Trueblood and others from California started showing up in the early 60s.

The steelhead fly-fishing history of the area was significantly impacted by three major groups of anglers and in the telling of the local history it is also an account of a much larger story. The three distinct groups that rose to the forefront as a result of my research were 1) some local and regional fishermen including Nez Perce Indians, 2) A California contingent and 3) a Pacific Northwest group from Seattle

Not many of the steelhead fly-fishermen that have contributed to the rich history of this area could be considered to be home grown. The majority of the anglers profiled in this book either live outside the area or have moved here since the 1970s. Among the more notable steelhead fly-fishermen that were born and raised in the Lewiston area and surrounding region include Paul Nolt, Elmer Crow, Bert Moffitt, Thorson Bennett, Levi Carson, Keith Stonebraker, Jeff Jarrett, and Bill Alspach.

The fishermen mentioned in the narrative below only represent a few that have fished the local waters but many of them are considered to be important from both a historical and local perspective.

Nez Perce and Locals

There is strong evidence that the Nez Perce had been fishing with what can only be described as fly-fishing techniques and gear for at least the last 200 years. Elders relate how hooks were fashioned out of bone and wood and how feathers of grouse and other birds were attached with animal glue. Lines from elk and deer sinew ensured that the catch could be pulled back in. When

the Nez Perce acquired the horse in the early 1700s fishing lines were made from woven horse hair and small pieces of buckskin were used as bait. Balls of horsehair known as sniggles that would become entangled in the fishes' many teeth were also used to catch salmon and steelhead

Two Nez Perce Indians that were born and raised on the Clearwater were among the first modern-day fly-fishermen to fish the Clearwater and North Fork/Kelly Creek country. Elmer Crow Sr. was a self-taught fly-fisherman and tier who became interested in the sport from reading *Field & Stream* articles in the 1940s and 50s, many of them authored by Ted Trueblood.

Elmer Sr. caught a Clearwater steelhead on a fly in 1951 and his son, Elmer Crow Jr. caught several fish in the late 1950s on the North Fork of the Clearwater and is the only person I know of that ever caught a steelhead on a fly in Kelly Creek.

Levi Carson is another Nez Perce steelhead fly-fisherman and like Elmer grew up on the river. He learned to fish on the Clearwater from his grandfather and he too remembers the large steelhead that used to show up on the upper North Fork and Kelly Creek drainages. He recalls that occasionally his grandfather would catch a steelhead on a fly on the upper North Fork when he was fly-fishing for cutthroat. Levi is one of the few anglers that have caught steelhead on a fly on the Ronde, Snake, and Clearwater in the same day.

Locals

Paul Nolt was the first steelhead fly-fisherman that I was able to verify that fished the local rivers and when I interviewed him at his home in Clarkston he was 86 years old. Paul passed away in November 2004. Paul and two of his friends, Norm Lawrence and Don Shook first fly-fished for steelhead at Shumaker Grade on the Grande Ronde beginning in the late 1930s. He was good friends with Ted Trueblood who would stop by the store to get information and talk about the bamboo fly rods that Paul started building in the 1940s.

Paul indicated that a local Lewiston doctor by the name of John Carsow fly-fished for steelhead on the Ronde starting in the early 1940s before the war. John on one occasion had told Keith Stonebraker about the six-pound rainbows he was catching on the Ronde during the fall and was wondering if the Game and Fish Department was going to continue stocking them. When Keith told him that those fish were actually steelhead, John didn't believe it.

Bert Moffett was an avid fisherman who was born near Orofino in 1920. Bert started tying his own flies in 1950 and his wife thinks that's when he started fly-fishing for steelhead. He spent 25 years as a mill worker in Northern California and while there fly-fished with Bill Schaadt for salmon on the Smith River. He moved back to Orofino in 1987. Jeff Jarrett said he was a very clever man and tied up some flies that were known as "wiggle flies." These flies resembled miniature hot shot lures and he even attached small diving blades to them.

Thorson Bennett was born in Elgin, Oregon in 1903 and fished the Grande Ronde from the late 50s to the early 70s.

North Fork of the Clearwater River in the fall.

Thorson was known for his Chappie fly and was good friends with Frank Cammack, Ted Trueblood, Wes Drain, and Bert Sumrow.

Keith Stonebraker is one of the few anglers who is native to the area. Keith caught his first steelhead on a fly (Fall Favorite) on the Clearwater in 1966 and has helped many of the established locals who have moved to the Lewiston Valley since the 1970s. Keith served on the Idaho Game and Fish Commission for 11 years and has been a strong advocate for fish restoration.

One of Keith's lifelong friends that he met at the University of Idaho in the late 1950s was Doug Venerka from Illinois. Keith and Doug have fished all over the world together and Doug built a summer home about ten years ago on the banks of the Clearwater. Doug in turn introduced fellow Chicagoan Sylvester Nemes to the local rivers.

Doug also introduced Alan Johnson to the Clearwater. Alan was a national fly casting champion and has fished the Clearwater about every other year since the late 60s. Keith thinks that Alan was the first person to use Bombers on the Clearwater.

Keith first met the late Jack Hemingway in 1965 who he described "as an exceptional fisherman," on the Firehole in Yellowstone Park. In later years Keith and Jack served together on the Idaho Game and Fish Commission. Jack purchased a

home above the Grande Ronde in 1970 and fly-fished the local waters into the mid 90s.

Although Perk Lyda was not a fly-fisherman, he was the first licensed guide on the Clearwater River in 1963. Perk guided several fly-fishermen over the years and he guided Duke Parkening and his family on the North Fork before Dworshak Dam was completed in 1973. That area is now buried 700 feet under water

Bill Alspach was a well-known steelhead fly-fisherman who passed away in 1997. He was born in Lewiston and started fly-fishing for steelhead in the early 70s. He is given credit for developing a very popular local steelhead fly know as the "Beats Me." Bill fished a lot with Craig Lannigan and LeRoy Hyatt.

Jeff Jarrett is another local fly-fisherman who has been a fly-fishing guide on the Clearwater since 1978 and spends at least 100 days on the Clearwater each year. Jeff is the proprietor of Jarrett's Guide Service out of Orofino. He is a professional fly tier and is one of the first to use articulated leech patterns on the Clearwater.

Palouse Connection

Bob and Beverly Black started fishing the Ronde in 1951 while they were attending school at the University of Idaho. Bob catches most of his fish with dry flies and Jimmy Green says that

Beverly has caught more steelhead than any other woman he knows, and more than most men.

Fenton Roskelly wrote several articles over the years about the local rivers in the Spokane newspapers. Fenton was friends with a writer by the name of Rex Gerlach who wrote the first article about the Grande Ronde in *Field & Stream* in 1966. Up until that time Ted Trueblood had written about the river but refused to name it, but Gerlach's article changed all that.

In the late 50s and early 1960s a few fly-fishermen from the Pullman/Moscow area began fishing the area, mostly the Grande Ronde. They included Benton Collins, Clark Hamilton, Jack Rogers, Alan Berryman, Don Brunell and Donald Satterlund. Benton Collins a farmer from Albion had his picture taken with a fish that was published in an article about the Grande Ronde in 1966 by Rex Gerlach.

Another fisherman that was good friends of Tom Morgan, Doug Venerka, and Keith Stonebraker was Gale House from Walla Walla. Gale has fished the Clearwater since 1970 and he fished the Grande Ronde in 1966. Gale met Ed Ward and Mel Leven on the Clearwater in the early 70s and Ed gave Gale his favorite pattern which was a Princeton Tiger. Gale used that fly almost exclusively for the next 10-15 years because it was such a good producer, and in 1987 caught a 45-inch, 25-pound fish with that pattern. His wife Dicksie started fly-fishing with him in 1980 and has caught several fish over the years.

In 1972 Dave Engerbretson and Dave Hansen from Moscow, ID began fishing the Ronde and Clearwater. Dave had been taught how to fly-fish from George Harvey when he attended the University of Pennsylvania in the 1960s. Dave in turn passed his knowledge of the local rivers down to Pullman artist Jim Palmershein and young John Toker who also attended the University of Pennsylvania and guided for Orvis on many of the East's spring creeks. John has established a reputation in a small amount of time as a top-notch steelhead fly-fisherman and Spey rod caster.

Indian paintbrush along the North Fork of the Clearwater River.

California Connection

One of the best fly-fishermen that this country has ever produced was northern California's Bill Schaadt. He mainly confined his fishing to such rivers as the Eel, Russian, and Smith, where he almost became a permanent fixture. His whole life was entirely devoted to the sport. Fly-fishing was an obsession with him. Bill died in 1996 and was elected to the Northern California's Fly-Fishing Hall of Fame in 1998.

Although Schaadt only fished once on the Clearwater that I'm aware of, his influence has radiated in all directions and the fly-fishermen he mentored have played a major role in the evolution of fly-fishing on the local rivers and in other places like the Florida Keys. Some of the anglers that Schaadt fished with and influenced included Ted Trueblood, Jim Green, Bob Weddell, Bert Moffett, Jim Adams, Woody Sexton, Walt Price, Mel Leven, Glen Brackett, and Russ Chatham.

Many including Weddell, Adams, Sexton, Walt (Dub) Price, Harry Wagoner, Jimmy Joseph and Glen Brackett also attended Humboldt State in the 1950s. Weddell, Adams, and Wagoner were roommates along with Jim Yokum who went on to become a noted big-game biologist in Nevada.

Many of the anglers mentioned above have had a significant influence on fly-fishing nation wide. Jim Adams and Bob Weddell were the first serious fly-fishermen to "put it all together," as Bob

likes to say, when they figured out how to catch chinook salmon on a fly on California's Smith River in 1956. Harry Wagoner went on to a career in fisheries in Oregon and Jimmy Joseph is the president of the International Tuna Commission. Glen Brackett pioneered the riffle hitch on the Clearwater and in time became co-owner of the Winston Rod Company with Tom Morgan.

Many of the Northern California contingent, like Jim Adams, Bob Weddell, Duke Parkening, Mel Leven, and Jim Green, were technically expert casters because of their affiliation with some of the casting clubs in that part of the country, the most notable being the Golden Gate Casting Club in San Francisco.

In 1954 Jim Adams became one of the first fly-fishermen from the west coast to visit the Florida Keys and check out the tarpon opportunities. Adams had learned to double haul from Walter Powell in 1949 and was one of the first fly-fishermen to use that technique in the Keys. While in the Keys, Adams became acquainted with such anglers as Joe Brooks and Ted Williams. As a result of Adam's efforts, other west coat anglers including Woody Sexton, Glen Brackett, Ed Schmidtman, Russ Chatham, Bob Weddell, Jimmy Green, and Bill Schaadt, followed.

Ted Trueblood fished with Bill Schaadt, Mel Leven and Jimmy Green on the Russian River and in later years Ted, Jimmy, Phil Luck and Duke Parkening fished together on the Henry's

Fork in Idaho and the Green River in Wyoming. Ted introduced the Grande Ronde to Claire Conley, Jimmy Green, Ed Ward, and Mel Leven in the early to mid 60s.

Jimmy Green made his presence felt in 1938 at the age of 19 when he represented the United States in the amateur division at the world fly-casting championships in Paris, France. He learned to cast at the Golden Gate Casting Club in San Francisco. He took first in all four events and later went on to become one of the finest rod builders and designers this country has ever produced, including the now-famous two-handed graphite rods he first built in the early 1980s.

Jimmy was good friends with Ted Trueblood and first fished with him on the Russian River in California in the 1950s. Ted invited Jimmy and Carol to fish the Grande Ronde in the mid 1960s. Jimmy and his wife Carol, a champion caster in her own right, moved to the Grande Ronde in the late 1980s. By then they had introduced the Ronde to several of their friends, including Dale Knoche, Fred Gray, Dick Teske, Bob Strobel, Phil Lund, Doug Merrick and Harry Lemire.

Ed Ward was the husband of actress Jane Wyatt and soon others from the Disney studio were fishing the Ronde and Clearwater in the early 60s, including Milt Kahl, Mel Leven, Terry Glykening, Duke Parkening, Ken Peterson, and Ken Anderson. Parkening was so taken with the fishing and hunting opportunities in northern Idaho that he built a house on the Middle Fork of the Clearwater and moved there permanently in 1969. Duke and his family are some of the few fly-fishermen who had the opportunity to catch North Fork steelhead before Dworshak Dam was completed in 1978.

Bob Weddell meanwhile had moved from Northern California in 1965 and secured employment in Boise. A year later he moved to Orofino on the banks of the Clearwater. In his own words, "I went underground for several years" enjoying the splendid hunting and fishing that Idaho was known for in those years. Weddell as near as I can tell has probably caught as many steelhead on a fly as anyone ever has on the local rivers and the Clearwater for sure.

Weddell met up with an ex Humboldter by the name of Walt (Dub) Price on the Grande Ronde in 1967. At that time Walt was an artist in Seattle and a member of the Everett Flyfishing Club. Dub is given credit for first using the greased-line method on the Ronde. He instructed Weddell and many of his friends, including Bill Nelson and Lew Bel, to the greased line technique. Dub wrote about this new technique in a 1966 issue of *The Creel* published by the Flyfisher's Club of Oregon. Weddell immediately applied this new method on the Clearwater with great success.

Weddell taught this new method to Keith Stonebraker from Lewiston, Glen Brackett from Spokane, Tom Morgan from Clarkston, and Duke Parkening.

Glen Brackett, who was a friend of Bob Weddell's and also attended Humboldt State in the 50s, was one of the first to start riffle hitching on the Clearwater. He introduced Bill McAffee to the Clearwater in the early 70s. Bill was a brilliant fisheries biologist from Michigan who migrated out west and fished and guided in Yellowstone, the Henry's Fork and Argentina for several years and spent a lot of time exploring, and fishing uncharted territory in the Brook's Range in Alaska. He fished the Clearwater for almost 20 years before he was killed in a small plane crash in Alaska in 1991.

Pacific Northwest Connection

Shortly after World War II, Rick Miller from the Seattle area learned how to fly-fish for steelhead from his long-time friend Wes Drain. In October of 1945, Rick decided to explore the Grande Ronde River that he had seen depicted on maps. That trip was very successful and Rick who now resides in a home next to the Snake River has fished the area ever since. Rick was good friends with Ralph Wahl, Paul Ramlow, Wes Drain, Lee Wulff, Enos Bradner, and Walt Johnson. Many of these men and others fished with Rick on the Snake and Ronde.

Rick introduced his friend and fellow guide, Paul Ramlow to the Ronde in 1955. Paul showed up with his array of bamboo fly rods and still fishes with them today, including some rather heavy English bamboo two-handed rods. Ramlow fished with Wes Drain, Keith Stonebraker, Sylvester Nemes, Jack Hemingway, Lee Wulff and met Bill McMillan on the Ronde.

Rick was also friends with Ralph Wahl and fished with him on the Grande Ronde. Ralph was a noted fly-fisherman and photographer and there are several photos of fly-fishermen and of the Grande Ronde in some of the books that Ralph went on to write.

Rick was a member of the Everett Fly Club and in 1955 returned to the Ronde with Bill Nelson and Lew Bell. Other active members of the Everett club and other friends who fished the Ronde with Nelson for several years included Dick Denman, John Carleson, Walt Price, Marty Rijowski, and later Dick Padovan and Don Haines.

Nelson's group deserves special mention for several reasons. Lew Bell was a respected attorney who had quite a bit of clout with the Olympia political establishment and was instrumental in getting catch-and-release regulations instituted on the North Stillaguamish and the Grande Ronde.

Nelson's group is also credited with forming the Federation of Fly-fishermen in Eugene, Oregon in 1963. The idea to form that group originated on the banks of the Grande Ronde, around late-October camp fires. Rick Miller and Nelson also helped Ted Trueblood and Lee Wulff make some of the first made-for-television steelhead movies on the Grande Ronde in the late 1960s.

Nelson also made several of the first films that we have of the early days of fly-fishermen catching steelhead on a fly. Some of the fishermen that he has footage of include Lew Bell, Dick Denman, Wes Drain, Dub Price, and Ted Trueblood.

Nelson's group befriended a young 17-year-old neophyte fly-fisherman in 1957 by the name of Jake Gulke. Steelhead Jake who resides next to the Clearwater above Orofino has fished the local rivers and others ever since and is one of the area's most knowledgeable fly-fishermen. Jake fishes a lot in British Columbia and is renowned for his fly tying and enthusiasm for trying new patterns. Jake has introduced other anglers to the area including Gordie Olsen, Howie Kubick, Mike Ressa, Bill Baker, John Newberry and Brett Bond. John Newberry is from Chewelah Washington and has a reputation as a first-rate fly tier and has written articles about the Peacock Spider that he fishes almost exclusively.

Jake, Gordie, and Randy Shaffer became good friends with the Greens and have spent many hours with Jimmy building rods and Spey lines, and learning how to cast two-handed rods. They have done well in tournament casting competitions.

Angler Profiles
1930s

*P*aul Nolt who resides in Clarkston, Washington and at the tme of this interview was 86 years old is certainly one of the first anglers to catch steelhead on a fly on the Grande Ronde. Paul passed away in November of 2004. In the mid to late 30s Paul and two of his friends, Don Shook and Norm Lawrence, fly-fished for steelhead on the Grande Ronde at Shumaker Grade.

Paul learned to fly-fish at a very early age and went on to found Lolo Sporting Goods in Lewiston in 1955. He became good friends with Ted Trueblood over the years and Ted was always eager to see how Paul was progressing with his rod building.

Paul: I've lived in this area a long time for sure. I'm 86 now and I came here in 1925 when I was nine years old. I was born in South Dakota in 1916 and my father was a Methodist minister. I graduated from Lewiston High School in 1935.

Lewiston residents and friends of Paul Nolt on the Grande Ronde in the 1940s. Don Shook (left), Norm Lawrence (middle), Hugh Helpman (right).

The first time I fly-fished for steelhead was on the Grande Ronde in the 1930s. Our first trip was down Shumaker Grade. I remember we liked to have never got out of there. We had an old Model T Ford and we burned the bands out of it coming up the hill and had to carry five gallons of water to keep the radiator filled.

I must say that that first trip was only about a half attempt to fly-fish. It wasn't dry-fly-fishing. We were using a fly and occasionally we would get a fish. We used a wet Muddler Minnow that would sink. We didn't have floating lines. We would wax our lines to try to get them to float, but it didn't work very well. I fished with Don Shook on that first trip. His father had the Dodge garage in Lewiston. Norm Thompson also fished with us down there.

We never saw anybody else on those trips. We always had the river to ourselves. We didn't go down there too often. The road was bad and it was a horrendous trip. We would go down in the early fall.

When we first started there was only myself, Don Shook, and Norm Lawrence. Later my partner at the store, Hugh Helpman, fished a lot with us. In the 1940s before the war broke out a local doctor by the name of John Carsow started fly-fishing the Ronde, and in the mid 60s I hired a manager in the store from British Columbia by the name of Bill Jollymore who was a hell of a fly-fisherman.

There weren't very many fishermen period in those early days, not even bait fishermen. People were too hungry and trying to make a living. They didn't have time to go fishing. You were looked down on if you fished; people thought that you must be too lazy to work. You have to remember that people have a lot more leisure time today and can fish more. In the first place if you had a job you would be working a minimum of 60 hours a week. Most jobs were six or seven days a week.

In the late 1940s after the war, a few fly-fishermen from Spokane started showing up. That was the first time that I saw a man that could really handle a fly and had the equipment to do it. That was in 1946 on the Grande Ronde up around the Turkey Run down by the mouth.

I first started being aware of outsiders coming in to fly-fish for steelhead in the early 60s. A lot of them were from California.

The late Paul Nolt caught several steelhead on a Royal Coachman in the late 1930s.

Royal Coachman
(tied by Dave Clark)

Tail: Golden pheasant tippets
Butt: Peacock herl and scarlet floss
Hackle: Brown
Wing: White bucktail or calf tail

They were the first real avid steelheaders. Up until that time people would just catch a few fish here and there.

Ted Trueblood was in the store a number of times. Ted fished the Ronde in the early 60s. He would always stop in to see me because he was very much interested in the rod building I was doing. There was nobody building bamboo rods in those days. Ted invited me to go with him several times but I was always too busy in the store to go.

We used the standard hackle patterns like the Gray Hackle, the Queen of Waters, Royal Coachman, Muddler Minnow, and my favorite was a Willow. It was a gray fly that would float. The Skunks didn't come out till the 60s around here.

We also used grasshopper patterns to catch steelhead. I caught a few on them but my friend Don Shook caught a lot of steelhead on grasshoppers. Don fished more than I did because he had access to cars from his father's business.

In the 30s and 40s people would catch those large B-run fish by spearing or snagging. Spearing was legal in those days. Norm Lawrence and I tried to catch some of those big steelhead a few times in the late 30s and early 40s but I can only remember a few fish that I actually caught with the fly on top of the water. Most generally the fly would sink 2-3 feet under the surface and I don't consider that fly-fishing, but we did catch a lot of fish on those submerged flies.

1940s

Rick Miller was one of the first steelhead fly-fishermen who started fishing the Grande Ronde in 1948.

R ick Miller has been fly-fishing for steelhead in the Pacific Northwest for close to fifty years and has fished the Grande Ronde since 1945. Rick turned 82 in October 2002 and a day after his birthday caught a steelhead on the Grande Ronde with his good friend Paul Ramlow. Rick is one of the first fly-fishermen to catch a steelhead on a fly on the lower Grande Ronde.

Much of his adult life was spent as a ski guide, goldsmith and watercolor painter in Sun Valley, Idaho. He now lives along the Snake River above Asotin in a house he designed himself and built with much of the weathered basalt rock that is so common to the area. Rick was good friends with many famous fly-fishermen, including Ted Trueblood, Lee Wulff, Ralph Wahl, Bill Nelson, Wes Drain, Jack Hemingway, Jimmy Green, and Walter Johnson. He was instrumental in forming the Fly-fishing Federation with Bill Nelson and others in 1963.

Rick: I was a steelheader always searching for new water. I knew that there were a lot of fish that went up the Columbia, Snake, and Clearwater. I had heard about the rivers over here. I was anxious to fish the Clearwater because it had a magnificent run of large steelhead. The Clearwater had the biggest run of the largest steelhead on the coast. Upon further investigation, I heard a tributary of the Snake (Grande Ronde) that might have steelhead.

It was October of 1945 and I drove into Asotin at 7:00 in the evening. I asked some people about the area and they told me it was possible to drive 30 miles down the Snake River to the

Rick Miller

Grande Ronde. I started down that night but the road was really bad. It was nothing more than a wagon trail with deep ruts. I had a station wagon and most of the time I had to keep one tire in the center of the road so I wouldn't high center. A few times I had to get out and shovel dirt to keep from getting highcentered. It took me three hours to get to Heller's bar.

I parked at the river and slept in my car. The next morning I got up and started fishing with a sinking line and an Orvis bamboo impregnated rod. On my second cast I caught a fish and in one place I caught seven fish on seven casts and landed all of them. I quit at noon because I was bored and tired. I know it's hard to believe but you can't really appreciate a steelhead unless you have to work for it. The next day was Sunday and it was a repeat of the same thing. I caught lots of fish and quit at noon to do some exploring.

I didn't come back again till 1948. By then I had a new pickup and camper. At times the fishing was too good. It was unbelievable how many fish there were in that river. In 1948 I also stopped at the Clearwater for a couple of days and learned that there was some mean fish in the Clearwater.

After my first trip in 1945 I didn't tell anyone for a while. There was a group of us who belonged to the fly-fishing club out of Everett and I talked to Bill Nelson and Lew Bell about this area. Lew was practicing law in Everett and he was very protective of the fish. Others in that group included Dick Denman, Dick Padovan and Don Haines.

I tie my own flies and most of them don't have official names that I'm aware of. I just made them up myself. Most of my flies tend to be very sparse and I tie both dark and bright patterns. Once you get into bright patterns I don't think it makes much difference, because, although your dressings are altered here and there on the fly, the overall image is the same. That's what the fish gets most times, just an image. The same would hold true with the darker patterns.

I do think there is a time for dark and a time for bright, depending on the light of the day and so forth. If I get a grab I won't necessarily change patterns unless I think he got nicked. I don't fish surface patterns because I really prefer that silent underwater swing. I love that unseen pull. I still use a sink-tip line most of the time.

I met Lee Wulff in 1963 through the Federation of Fly-fishermen in Eugene that Nelson cooked up. Nelson got the idea for that organization from fishing over here. We were all in a bar in Everett one night at an Evergreen Club meeting and Nelson out of the blue said, "You know," he said, "what we should do is have a national federation of fly-fishermen and get all the fly clubs in the nation that are interested to join. Then we would have power and we could influence legislatures and everything."

We all agreed with it. Nelson went back to Eugene and started calling people like Ted Trueblood, Lee Wulff, Jimmy Green, and other notables in the fishing fraternity, most of them back east. He told them they were going to have a national meeting in Eugene, Oregon on such and such a date and would they please come and be guest speakers.

Nelson had a good ploy that he used to get all those big names to attend. He would call one of them and mention that a lot of the other well-known fly-fishermen were going to attend before he had commitments from most of them. It worked!

Bill called me and told me about the upcoming meeting. He said, "There's another thing we could do that I think would really be great."

For the Everett Club I had made them a club pin out of gold, so now Nelson is telling me about all these powerful guest speakers that we are going to have and asked me if I could prepare a memento for each of them.

I said, "Good idea, Bill, you bet I will." So I made gold flies, steelhead fly patterns, one for each of the speakers.

Wes Drain Story

My dear friend Wes Drain was a magnificent fly-fisherman and he was very secretive. Holy smoke, this was a man who wouldn't even kid about the truth. He wouldn't stray from the truth even to kid just a little. He stayed right clear the way it was, straight on the line. He told me about a fish he lost on the Wind River.

He had scouted the fish and got a visual on them. He saw three steelhead in this pool right where they were supposed to be along the ledge.

He said he figured two of them were small somewhere around 8-9 pounds. The third one looked to be about 15 pounds. Now, Wes was a little bit off on his judgment. He could not get close to them. He was a long ways up above them. He had to try and judge their size by looking at their backs.

Well, he fished to them and that big one took. He fought it in that pool for a half hour. He got it up next to the sand bar and had it grounded several times, but one swish and its back out again. He didn't dare run the leader into his guides, he used 20-ft leaders. He said he couldn't trust the knots to go through the guides.

He backed up as far as he could, pointed the rod at it and was prepared if it did turn to arch the rod quickly. He got it up and got it grounded and said the back was out of the water. He laid the rod down and ran down there real quick and he got it in his arms. He said, he had it but it was slipping all over and he couldn't get to shore with it and it got away. He said it was a big fish, enormous, he said.

I said, "Was it 20?"

"Oh yeah," he said.

"Was it 25?"

"Yeah," he said.

"Would it have went 30?" I said.

"More than that," he said.

I said, "Would I be close if I said 40?"

He said, "Yeah, you would be pretty close."

He said it was like the biggest king salmon he had caught at Neah Bay. It was a huge fish.

Snake River Boat Accident

I told Wes about the Ronde and he started coming over for several years. One year in the early 70s we had a real bad accident. John Carlson brought some McKenzie boats over.

We decided to float the Snake. We had movie cameras and we were going to film us catching steelhead. Now I have always heard that a McKenzie river boat was the whitewater craft of all crafts. It's built like a damn rocking chair leg.

Well, we started out and Carlson is on the oars. We put in at Heller's Bar.

Wes Drain and I are in the boat with him. Wes always wore a large fly vest that protruded out a long ways in back. One time

Anglers in this photo include Rick Miller and Lee Wulff photographed on the Grande Ronde while filming a movie for the American Sportsman in 1967.

Dark unnamed fly
(tied by Rick Miller)

Tail: Yellow hackle tip
Tag: Gold
Body: Orange chenille with silver rib
Wing: Orange and yellow bucktail
Collar: Golden pheasant feather
Hackle: Orange and yellow

Rick Miller tied his own unnamed flies in both dark and light patterns.

in Canada I put a 15 pound rock in it and he carried it all day and didn't know it. He took it in good spirit when he found out.

Over in the other boat were Bill Nelson, Lew Bell, and Dick Denman. Nelson had a camera and I had my special custom-built Bell and Howell turret model 16 mm.

We started out. I had told them there was only one bad rapid on the river and it's only down the river a half mile. That's all the conversation we had, because Nelson has seen the river his whole life.

Anyhow, you had to go through the channel on the far side to avoid the rapid. Even the tour boats went there. No one went through the middle of that Captain Lewis Rapid. The thing that makes it a dangerous rapid is that at the bottom there are huge rocks creating huge curl backs at the surface. When you look down on that rapid from the road it looks very benign, but boy, watch out when you get into it.

Nelson's boat went through on the side and got through just fine, but that idiot Carlson went down the middle, and I thought, Oh no, we're going into it. The next thing I know is that I'm wet. The boat barely got over the first rapid but the second rapid turned the boat completely upside down. This is all on Bill Nelson's video camera. It shows 3 guys dropping out head first with all the gear.

Wes and I are in full regalia for fishing because we were going to fish down river. Well, now I'm going to the bottom of the river. I have 18 pounds of camera locked on my wrist and that thing was acting just like an anchor and I went right to the bottom. I'm struggling; I had instinctively taken a deep lung full of air before my head went into the water.

I thought, don't get panicky, you've still got air. I finally got the camera off my wrist but I knew I couldn't swim with it so I had to let it go. When I came up to the surface, I couldn't believe it, I was under the boat. The boat was coming down through the top of the rapid. I'm on the bottom of the river struggling with a camera, not even moving for a few seconds and when I did come up I hit the boat, it was perfect.

The boat had floatation tanks in it so it wouldn't sink, but it was upside down. I just hung on to the boat, that's all I could do. I went down river with it. Meanwhile, Wes who was a very stocky, heavy man was in big trouble. He had short white hair, kind of a long butch cut and it was white.

Nelson and his boat came over as fast as they could at the bottom of the rapid to help in any way they could. Well, Carlson, the big strong kid, all he did was just get wet, he just swam ashore. So Nelson and Lew Bell came over and couldn't see any of us, except for Carlson. They couldn't see me or Wes.

So they figured if anything gets to the rapid it will be at the bottom. They made another swing and came across down at the bottom of the rapid. Down there, as they were peering over the edge of the boat they saw that white head down under the water.

So Nelson went over head first and Lew Bell held onto his ankles and he went down and he got a hold of Wes's hair and pulled him out. They took him ashore and Dick Denman pumped him out. He was just fine at dinner that night.

Then they had only me to worry about. They figured that I had drowned. There was no sign of me. They went down river and there was nobody swimming or anything. I went down river about 6 miles hanging onto the boat, hoping somebody would do something to help me. I drifted by one of those little beach coves where some guys had just went ashore. They had a pretty big craft and they saw me out there and they jumped in that boat and came roaring out there and hauled me aboard and towed the boat in too. Then I hitchhiked back up to the camp on the Ronde.

Lee Wulff Film

I became good friends with Lee Wulff. He called me one time. He was doing TV stuff. Lee was working with the "American Sportsmen Series." He asked me if he came out could we get a good steelhead film.

I said, "Yes, Lee, but I would have to swear you to secrecy. I will take you to a river that has lots of fish, but you can't name the river in the film."

Well, he finally agreed to that, but he didn't like it. I wasn't very enthused but agreed to help him. We got some good film. This was in the early 70s. We stayed in my camper. Part of it was a fiasco, one of the sponsors for the film was the Garcia Tackle Company, and they sent along an actor to be in the film.

He was a dumb guy, about 25 years old, and he was just a clown and he couldn't fish. He could mimic us a little bit; some-times he could get a 30 foot cast. I would fish above him and follow him down. As soon as I would hook a fish I would pass him the rod and Lee would turn the camera on him.

We both had cameras. If the fish stayed on long enough I would go to shore and get my camera. We managed to get some pretty good film that way. Dammit, I never could get any film of Lee with a fish because he refused to fish for steelhead like we fished for steelhead.

He fished for them the same way he did for Atlantic salmon. He would throw upstream and let the fly sink and come down on a dead drift any old which way, it didn't matter and he could not catch a fish. We were up there a couple of days and I kept telling him what he should do because he kept saying, "How in the hell do you keep hooking fish all the time and I can't get into a fish?" I said, "Well, Lee, you're not fishing for them the way you have to fish for steelhead."

I explained to him, what you need is to have that fly land unobtrusively, sink and then let it drift the same speed as the water downstream and then of course it will start to swing and come across. I said, "You will either get the fish as it starts to drift or as it makes the swing. All through that swing, just hang on, because your fly will be behaving perfectly, head upstream and it will be swinging. That's what they like."

In 1986 I got a big one up at Heller's Bar. I was fishing with my friend Bernie. He hooked into a big fish. The thing arched out of the water and it looked like a tarpon. I yelled up to Bernie, "You've got a big fish on." and he said, "I know it!"

Pretty soon the fish got tired of thrashing around and starts his downstream work, so Bernie had to come on down. He took

Bright unnamed fly
(tied by Rick Miller)

Tag: Gold followed by pink
Body: Orange chenille with silver rib for 1st third followed with black chenille
Wing: Natural bucktail
Collar: Golden pheasant feather
Hackle: Dark brown and red

it down to the boat launch where there was a big holding pool. The ramp was cross cleated and it ran into the water. After a while he came back up, he had measured it but he couldn't weigh it. It was 42 inches long and the girth was in proper proportions to the length.

While he was gone I had hooked and lost a big one. Bernie came back up and right away he had another one and again he ended up at the boat ramp. After a half hour he is back up there again and he said it was a twin of the first one.

Well, I hooked another one and this one stayed on. I ended up down at the ramp too. When I got it to the point where it wanted to lay over I slid him up on the ramp, but still keeping him wet. I tried to weigh him but my Deliar scale went right to the bottom. I couldn't weigh him. I measured him; he was a 43-inch fish.

It had a hell of a girth and I took a few scales to get his life story. About that time a guide boat came into the dock with three clients. They were all talking and looking at the fish on the ramp. I had just unhooked it and moving it back and forth in the water, and one of them said, "What are you doing?"

I said, I'm making sure that the gills are functioning well so that when I release him I will be assured that he's returned to the wild in good condition."

He said, " Don't release him, I'll take him."

I said, "Well, this fish has struggled for two months, traveled 800 miles and went through 9 dams to get here, he's going to go up and spawn."

Well, the guide come over and said, "What does it weigh?"

I said, I couldn't weigh it because the scale was too small.

"God," he said, "that's some fish. I've been guiding on this river for 18 years and have never seen a fish like that." He asked me to just keep it a little longer, so he could get an official scale. He did and that fish weighed 29 pounds 4 ounces. We had hooked four of those fish that morning and landed three of them.

About this time the same guy came back over and said, "I'll buy him from you."

I said, "No, you don't have enough money."

The guide and I got to theorizing about the fish. Nobody had ever seen a fish that big. I said I lost one just like it. I think they were some of the original Clearwater stock that didn't go straight ahead, they made a wrong turn. The whole school of them came up the Snake. The guide agreed, they had to be Clear-water fish. I remember reading about a 34-pounder which was a record for the Clearwater.

Above right: Rick Miller caught his first steelhead on a fly on the Grande Ronde in 1948. He now resides in a home he built along the Snake River.

Below: Anglers on the Grande Ronde in 1967. Left to right, Ray Presgoda, Lew Bell, Wes Drain, Lee Wulff, Rick Miller.

Heron rookery on the Snake River near Clarkston, Washington.

1950s

Bob and Beverly Black of Salem, Oregon have been fishing the Grande Ronde since 1951.

Bob and Beverly Black

Bob and his wife Beverly have been fly-fishing the Grande Ronde and Snake for steelhead since the early 1950s and know that body of water as good if not better than most who fish there. Jimmy Green told me that he thinks Beverly has caught more steelhead than any other woman who has fished there, and more than most men. They reside in the Portland area, but spend most of their summers at their second home on Hayden Lake in northern Idaho.

Bob: My wife and I both attended the University of Idaho in the 1940s. We heard about the Grande Ronde from the sporting goods store in Moscow. They sold Beverly and me our first rods, nine-foot South Bend bamboo rods.

The first time I fished the Ronde was in 1951 at the place we called Rattlesnake. I guess today people call it Bogan's. It was the first time I had ever tried to catch steelhead on a fly. I had a Pleuger Medalist Reel and a Newton silk line that sunk. We were excited on the first try but we had no idea what to expect. I started out with a Skykomish Sunrise which I had tied after reading Enos Bradner's book *Northwest Angling*. I have a book that tells the history of that fly. In those days we really overdressed our flies.

There was a time when you could almost catch all the fish you wanted, catch and release as fast as you can. It was really a thrill. I can remember hooking 47 fish one day. I don't even try to do that any more. If I can get two or three I stop and give up the water to someone else.

When we first started fishing we figured we had to be down deep. I was casting up and letting the fly come down on a natural

drift using a full-sink line. I caught an awful lot of fish using that method. Those fish would pick that fly up on the dead drift if it was down near the bottom.

I started using a Muddler in 1955 and Bill Nelson showed me how to do a riffle hitch.

"Put a half hitch on that Muddler," he said.

Man that made all the difference in the world. I caught a lot more fish when that Muddler was making that wake. We learned grease lining in a magazine. I like to cast 3/4 down stream and have that fly come across the current. The fish will hit many times with a very short drift. We normally use 8-pound-test leaders and sometimes we use 6-pound test. We make our own tapered leaders. We never set a hook on steelhead.

I use a lot of surface flies. It seems to work better over here. I have fished a lot of the west-side rivers but I catch more fish on waking Muddlers on the Ronde. When I come over here I use a floating line and a dry fly. It's a lot more fun. I use a cut down Muddler, no tail with a riffle hitch.

Beverly: I always use a floating line regardless of the temperature. I have never used a sink-tip. My favorite fly is a Bucktail Coachman. I use that almost exclusively in size 4. I have caught steelhead however on a number 14 fly. I saw this great big rock

Beverly Black, who has fished the Grande Ronde with her husband since the early 1950s, has caught more steelhead on a fly than most anglers according to Jim Green.

Bob Black loved to fish tailless Muddler Minnows on the surface.

Muddler Minnow with no tail
(tied by Bob Black)

Body: Gold tinsel
Wing: Brown turkey wing
Head and collar: Deer hair spun and clipped

The Bucktail Coachman is Beverly Black's favorite steelhead pattern.

Bucktail Coachman
(tied by Bob Black)

Tail: Red hackle fibers
Body: Peacock herl
Hackle: Brown
Wing: White Bucktail

on the Ronde one day and cast that small fly behind it and skittered it around behind it and up he came. That was one of my biggest thrills catching that steelhead on a small dry fly. When it comes to patterns, it doesn't really matter what you use. I like the Kalama Special and the Green Butt Skunk.

Another favorite fly I use is a strip of black rabbit fur tied with a bead head. I caught a beautiful Grande Ronde fish on it and it was the only fly I had any luck with that particular day and I went up to the Greens home later. Jimmy wanted to check something out on the rod and he took that fly and ripped it off and I haven't seen it since. I told him that he owes me a fly.

Bob: In 1951 on the way back home we stopped in at a shop in Yakama to see what kind of flies would work on the Klickitat. They had a fly that consisted of red calves tail tied all around the hook and then they put shrimp on it. So I tied a red calf-tail body and I hate to tell you this but I put a bead on it. You can't beat that fly for steelhead if you want to go deep. No tail, just a calf-tail body.

Beverly: If Bob gets a hit he will change flies many times but I won't. I will usually go upstream a little bit and try again with the same fly.

Bob: It's a waste of time really to change flies but I do it anyway. I use the Paul Young parabolic cane rod, it was built in 1951 and that is what I have used all these years. I use a 7- and 8-weight line on it.

Beverly: My favorite water is the lower Ronde. Its tricky wading because of the bedrock and it's up and down but it's still my favorite. I started fishing in 55. When one of those fish would hit and you would be standing out in the middle of the water, it was the biggest thrill in the world. You feel so free, I can't describe it, it's just great.

I still remember that first fish. I was standing out in the middle of the river. My daughter Sherry was behind me on the bank. I just cast out and this fish hit and my rod just doubled over and that fish took off downstream and it was soon into my backing and I didn't know exactly what to do and I lost him because I didn't know what I was doing. From that point on I was hooked and we tried to get down there as often as we could.

Ronde Experience

Beverly: I was fishing the lower Ronde in 1991 with Bill Reynolds from Redmond, Washington. He is the steelhead representative on "The Osprey" newsletter. We started out one morning and I cast first and caught a fish. Then he cast and caught a fish. We did this until we both had caught seven fish apiece. That always stands out to me. I was using that Bucktail Coachman and Bill was using a dark fly.

Bob: Sometimes guys at the mouth of the Ronde would catch a big fish. I had a friend who caught an 18-pounder there. It was probably a Salmon River fish. Contrary to other rivers, the very first steelhead we would start catching on the Ronde between the 14th and 21st of September would be beautiful hens. They would be 26-29 inches. Then pretty soon the 24-inch bucks would show up. You could get a 30-inch fish but that was big, 27 inches was probably closer to the average. Those were the native Grande Ronde fish and all of that has now changed. They were pretty mean fish; those little devils would give you a bad time.

Bill Nelson and Friends

Bill Nelson with a Grande Ronde steelhead. Bill and his group of friends fished the Ronde during the first week of October, starting in the mid 1950s, for many years. Bill was instrumental in forming the Federation of Fly Fishers.

Bill Nelson and his group have contributed a lot to the fly-fishing history of the Grande Ronde. Bill and his friends have fished the Ronde in early October since the mid 1950s and were some of the first ones to start using floating lines and surface flies.

Members of the original group were Bill Nelson, Lew Bell, and Rick Miller. Others that also fished with them extensively included Wes Drain, Walt Price, John Carleton, Dick Padovan, and Don Haines. Walt Price was responsible for introducing the greased-lined technique to the area and Lew Bell was an attorney that helped introduce catch-and-release regulations on the lower Grande Ronde. Bill Nelson was the principal organizer of the Fly-fishing Federation which began in 1963 in Eugene, Oregon. The idea to form that organization had its roots during those October trips to the Ronde.

Nelson: Our group started fishing the Ronde together in the 1950s but when I was at school at Washington State I had fished the Ronde in 1948-49 by myself. I went down there a couple of times, I didn't do too well. I didn't catch any steelhead, but I did real well catching bass.

The group of us from Everett started fishing the Ronde in 54-55. We did a lot of exploring in those days. The first time a group of us went it was with Rick Miller and Lew Bell.

Dub Price would camp with us on occasion in our first couple of years on the Grande Ronde. One evening I can remember someone saying, I've got to take a steelhead home.

So Dub says, "I'll go down and catch you one." He went down to the river and caught a steelhead on his first cast.

We fished the lower parts of the Ronde in October and would spend 10 days there. We started out sleeping in the back end of a camper and then went to tents and finally we got a pop-up trailer. We fished the Ronde through the heights of it and have known days when it was not unusual to catch fish on the fly that were 12- to 14-pound summer-run fish as we called them.

Nelson: Once Rick Miller showed us what to do we started doing a lot better. Up until that time I was just flailing away. After a few years we started using floating lines and grease lining with surface flies. I skated a Muddler one day in a pool without ever moving my feet and landed 17. Bob Black didn't believe those fish could be caught on a dry fly so one day I showed him. He watched one fish in the clear water come to a skating fly 11 times. They came after a floating fly on the Ronde and the Snake early in the day and late in the afternoon before dark. A floating fly worked in eddy type water and quiet pools.

Those early fish were something else. They would come to the surface. They were like fry almost the way they would take a fly. I have a case on my wall filled with flies tied in the 60s that guys fished with on the Ronde. These flies are a little different. Dub Price was the one that tied the sparse fly and they were good. I would steal a lot of them; I caught more fish on stolen flies than I did on my own.

Denman: I'm a firm believer that the pattern doesn't really matter. We all have our favorites and because you fish your favorite better than 50% of the time, that's when you catch fish and we credit the fly and not the fact that's what we have been using the most.

I liked to fish with a Muddler on a floating line and flies with a lot of grease. I also used variations of the Woolly Worm. We used wet flies, anything with red and yellow combinations like a Skykomish Sunrise, Stillaguamish Sunset, a Stillaguamish red fly. Spider patterns in gray and yellow were excellent.

Nelson: After about the fourth year, I always used a dry fly. Dub Price and I would get up early in the morning and skate flies. Skating is not grease lining. Grease lining is mending and putting it where you want it, it's a wonderful way to fish. We did it on the Umpqua before we came over here.

Dub actually refined it and helped me through it and then we started doing the riffle hitch. We did it with the wet flies to begin with. I was so excited about it I couldn't stand it, so I went and got a regular Muddler and greased it, put floatant on it and then skated across these little areas. It was hard to believe. It was like a fall caddis and no one really picked up on it except Dub. Then he passed on the information to us.

No one would believe us. We used to do a lot of casting just to see if we could get a rise. I didn't care if they took it. I wanted to see that rise. One day Lew and I came down the river together and we got to a slot, they named it Nelson's Slot. Anyway, we got there, Lew was waist deep in water and a fish came up to my dry fly 7-8 times.

Muddler Minnow
(tied by Paul Ramlow)

Tail: Brown turkey wing
Body: gold tinsel
Wing: Brown turkey wing
Head and collar: Deer hair spun
and clipped

Bill Nelson fished Muddler Minnows for several years with great success on the Grande Ronde.

Finally he got it. Up to that time Lew hadn't believed us. Lew was using a stripping basket for his line but it didn't have holes in it. He was reeling in his line and he had a little trouble with the basket, he wanted to put on a dry line. When he saw what happened he wanted to try it. He reeled it in and instead of dumping the water out into the river he ended up dumping the water into his waders. He was laughing; he got that cold water down under you know where.

Federation of Fly Fishers

Nelson: We had talked about forming a national federation for a couple of years while we were fishing for steelhead on the Ronde. Lew Bell, Dick Denman, Rick Miller and sometimes other people would talk about it. We were the primary group that would go up and camp on the Grande Ronde.

Denman: One evening we were laying in our sleeping bags looking up at the stars and seeing the first Sputnik there on the river. We were drinking the last bit of Scotch we had before we went home and we started talking about why we couldn't put all these fly-fishing clubs together. I said to Lew who was a pretty good lawyer in putting companies together and I said, "Why don't we get all of these fly-fishing clubs under one banner and we would have more clout where we could show up in Olympia, Washington with a membership of 25,000 or some large number."

We talked about that all night till each one of us fell asleep and the fire went out. That was the conclusion that we came to. There was a lot of discussion about what it should be called. I think Nelson and Bell came up with the name. I didn't particularly like it, that FFF thing. It was literally formed and put together that night.

Nelson: I became president of the Everett Fly-fishing Club and I tried to put it across to them but then I got transferred to Eugene, Oregon. I thought, well, hell I am going to try and do it from here. I helped form the McKenzie Fly Club. I missed the camaraderie that I had in Everett. The guys here in Eugene kind of jumped on it with me and we formed the club. We enlisted the

support of fishermen like Lee Wulff, Ted Trueblood, and Jimmy Green to get started.

Fishing Ronde

Denman: I guess the most exciting part for me was the first time I was fishing with a dry fly in the late 60s. We got some pictures of fish hitting the dry fly and showed it to the Theodore Gordon Club back east.

I think that first fish that I caught on the dry fly was at the last bend where the Ronde flows into the Snake. I was not experimenting but was determined that there were steelhead lying in those rocky areas. It made sense to me. I was able to get one cast that floated the fly right down around the edge of a rock and all hell broke loose. I guess I'll never forget that.

Padovan: My favorite fly was a Muddler. I also used the low-water salmon flies too, but generally, I used a Muddler. Dub Price tied a good Muddler. Dub taught us how to grease line and that's the way we fished unless we were skating Muddlers.

I took a fellow that had never been there before and we fished for two days. I put him in the run above me. I told him to cast right by a certain rock and showed him how to skate a Muddler. Pretty soon I heard him whistling, so I walked back up and he told me, that a fish had come 12 times to the fly. He had hooked it once. I told him to drift it a little bit more and then skate it and he did and a fish took it. It was a nice fish, bigger than normal, around 10 pounds. As soon as he landed that one I got back in there because I figured there had to be more than one fish. I immediately hooked two fish.

The one fish I remember the most is when Lee Wulff was there making a film. Lee couldn't catch any fish. Lew Bell kept saying every night as we were eating, "I can get you a fish." So finally he headed out. I knew exactly where he was going to go. Lewie skated a Muddler in a couple of those slicks and a fish came and took it, and they kept that fish on all day. They used it in the film. They tied it up along the shore when they went to lunch. I couldn't believe it.

Paul Ramlow

Paul Ramlow with two Grande Ronde steelhead caught in 1955. Paul fishes exclusively with bamboo rods and is still active.

Paul Ramlow is a spry 82 year old who has fly-fished for steelhead in this area since 1955. He only fishes with bamboo rods, many of them two-handed. He caught 37 fish in the fall of 2001 with his 14-foot 21-ounce Sharps bamboo rod that was made in England. Paul was a ski and fishing guide in Sun Valley, Idaho and people that he guided over the years included Lawrence Welk, Rod Sterling, and Lee Wulff.

Paul: I grew up near a lake in Saratoga, New York. When I was 18 and got wheels I started to fish the Battenkill which was about 40 miles from home and the Au Sable River. I fished it in the mid 30s when Ray Bergman was still fishing there.

I was a tool and die maker in Schenectady, New York for a while. In 1950 I decided I would give everything up and go out west and teach skiing. So I came to Sun Valley and became a ski instructor. In the summer after a year or so in Sun Valley, I became a fishing and hunting guide in the summer.

Whenever I could get away, I would drive up to Lewiston and fish the Ronde mostly. I first came in 1955; Rick Miller showed me the river and we fished for three days. On that first trip he took me out and would say, "Okay, cast in front of that rock," and I would. I think I landed thirteen steelhead in two and a half days. Rick would just point out where he wanted me

Fall Favorite
(tied by Paul Ramlow)

Body: Silver tinsel
Hackle: Red
Wing: Orange bucktail

The Fall Favorite is a popular steelhead pattern and one of Paul Ramlow's favorites.

to cast. In fact, he didn't fish at all until we were ready to leave and he caught one.

After that I came up every time I could. It's a 450-mile trip. I would come over in October and drive all night to fish three days and drive all night to get home. I did this for several weeks in a row every year. I drove a red Trans Am, I used it for driving and fishing. It was a hard car to get in and out with waders.

We were using full-sink lines in the early days. I used sinking lines longer than everybody else and Keith Stonebraker was always after me to use a floater. Finally, I did and I found out that I could catch just as many on a floater. I like to use a lot of the old-fashioned patterns or at least ones that look old fashioned. I like to use a number 6 fly tied on a 1/0 hook. It's a low-water pattern that's really heavy and sparse.

I like Fall Favorites, and all kinds of Spey flies with the long hackles with hardly any body at all. Sometimes I will fish with small hooks, eights and tens but not very often. For a while I fished a lot with a riffling dry fly. I found out it wasn't that much fun, you could put a wet fly on and fish it a couple of inches below the surface and get the same reaction, so I haven't done that too much lately. I found I could do pretty well with the smaller wet flies close to the surface.

I use traditional flies and use cane rods. I have 25 cane rods. They are all functional, they all work fine. Three of them are two-handed rods. I also have 3 vintage cane rods that go back to pre World War I. I think the bamboo is great and has an action of course that you can't duplicate with graphite.

A friend of mine just died, Paul Brown a rod maker from West Yellowstone. The last 8-9 years he came and fished with me here. He built wonderful rods. He worked with Jimmy Green at Fenwick. I was with him when he died, and his family was very grateful and they gave me the pick of any rod that he had and Paul made some very unusual rods that others said were too soft for Spey rods, long and too light of line.

The one I picked is 16 1/2 foot for an 8 line and it's a beautiful rod. In fact, I gave up my bamboo and for the last 4 years I have been using Paul's rod. I've taken over one hundred steelhead on it. It's just wonderful.

Around 1992 I wanted to learn to Spey fish and with Paul's help I bought a cane rod, I sent to England for it, a 14-foot Sharps for a 10 or 11, it weighs 21.5 oz. I used that almost steady for three years, I kept plugging away with it, it's not too easy. It wasn't too forgiving.

I really enjoy it, especially now. I'm 82, now I will only stand in the water for four hours and that means I have to be away from home for six hours. That's good enough for me, 4 hours. You'd be surprised at how long you can keep your fly in the water during four hours time Spey casting. You can keep that fly out there forever. With a one-handed rod you can't. I love fishing the Snake, especially with the Spey rod. A long Spey rod makes it great.

Years ago if I had a pull I would often change patterns but nowadays I'll shorten my line and fish again and move down. That's it. I won't fool with it, because something usually happens within several casts.

I caught a large fish on the Clearwater in the 70s. It was the year when we couldn't keep any fish, and I caught one that was 44 inches long. It had a girth of 21 inches or something like that. It was a male; it was probably a 25-pound fish, that's what Keith Stonebraker told me, he had seen those fish in the hatchery.

Jake Gulke

Jake Gulke has been fly-fishing for steelhead on the local rivers since he was 17 years old. Jake was mentored by Bill Nelson and Lew Bell on the Grande Ronde.

Jake: I was fishing at a lake near Dillon, Montana a few years ago and the local sheriff came and got me. He wouldn't tell me what was up. I figured one of my family members had died or something. He told me to call the Clearwater County sheriff, so I did. The sheriff informed me that my house had burned down. I asked him if the neighborhood kids or anyone else had been hurt and when he said no, I hung up the phone and went back to fishing for the next three days. I figured there was nothing to come home for.

That about sums it up when you talk about Jake Gulke, also known as Steelhead Jake and the President of the Grande Ronde, a name that was given to him by Paul Ramlow. Jake lives above Orofino close to the Middle Fork of the Clearwater and he has fished for steelhead all over the western United States, Alaska, and Canada.

Jake: My dad used to haul Canadian cattle down here in Asotin County and that's when I first saw the Grande Ronde. I forget who in the hell he sold some bulls to on the Grande Ronde, but that's when I first saw that stream. I watched them fly-fishing it one time when I came over with my dad and wished that I could do it too.

Orange and Black
(tied by Jake Gulke)

Tag: Silver tinsel
Body: Black
Rib: Silver tinsel
Beard: Black saddle
Wing: Orange calf or
   hackle fibers

Jake Gulke fished an Orange and Black almost exclusively in his early years.

I first fished the Ronde in 1957 when I was still in high school. I ran away from home to go fishing. That's when I met Bill Nelson, Don Haines, Dick Denman, Marty Rijowski, John Carlson, and Lew Bell. Nelson and all of those guys were some of the first ones to fly-fish down there, way before anybody else.

I remember how I first met Nelson. I was fly-fishing down at the mouth. I was at the tail end of the run and the scrap iron throwers were reeling in and the lures would go right by me. I was out there wading and they didn't like it so they hooked me in the boot. They told me that all fly-fishermen had to fish upriver.

So I went up the river and saw Nelson and those guys. I told Nelson what happened. I had broken off the guy's lure and it was still in my boot and I put it on my vest. Nelson said, "They what?" It was evening and they were drinking gin and they got mad and Haines and Carlson went back down there to kick some ass. They would have straightened out that guy really quick.

That's how it got started. I had a drink of gin with them. They asked me if I had ever hooked a fish and I said no, but I'm going to. I was around every day and they knew that I was eventually going to catch one. Bill would laugh and tell me to keep working that water.

I was crazy over fishing. Nelson liked me for some reason. He said, "You wanna catch one, go fish there in the evening."

So I did and bingo I caught my first fish. Then I learned to fish the other holes. Haines would tell me not to fish them because it was dangerous. That dirty son of a gun would do that to me. So one day I went down there and caught a bunch of fish. It was water that nobody would fish because it was shallow. A

dry line is perfect for those conditions. I thought at the time, ha, ha Haines, I got your ass now.

In those days we used a lot of pure brown flies. No one ever used to use pure blue, but I do that now. Dick Zane gave me a copy of Wood's book on greased-lined fishing, that was fantastic and I got a lot of flies out of that.

I started tying all kinds of flies. Bill Nelson would always steal grasshoppers from me, but he would teach me a lot. Nelson loved to catch those fish with grasshoppers. These were all 5- to 6-pound wild fish. They are not there anymore. Those fish were aggressive, they were like a trout.

One day a mayfly hatch came on in October. They were little blue ones; I don't know what they were. Blue-winged olives or some darned thing. So I tied up that mayfly pattern.

Nelson said those fish went crazy for those flies. It was the 10th of October and he hooked seventeen steelhead on a dry and broke just about all of them off because he was using #14 hooks and 2- to 3-pound leaders.

I started fishing with an O and B, orange and black. The Thor was Don Haines's favorite fly. It's got a red and white hackle. I liked the Skunk which was a traditional pattern, it was a good fly. I changed a lot over the years as new materials came available. I always thought that big fish liked big flies. It was all a process of learning. No one really knew which fly was the best. Now I use blue flies. That's all I fished last year (2001), blue, period.

I think I was one of the first guys to start fishing with blue Flashabou. What made us do a lot of changing was the water conditions on the Ronde. High and muddy some days. So I started using flashy flies when the river was muddier than hell. If the river was clear I could fish behind guys with the little stuff I used and I mean number 12's, little bitty stuff and catch fish. One year I went to a Blue Charm and did fine.

I've caught a lot of fish in the dark. We learned this from Nelson, on cloudy days the fish run closer to shore, they feel safer. People say dark day/dark fly, bright day/bright fly. It doesn't matter.

You talk to steelheaders, they all have a favorite pattern. Me, I don't care. I learned that from Dick Zane. I stopped at my mother's place one time and she wanted to see my steelhead flies, so I took them out and showed her and she oohed and aahed. I'll be darned if I didn't leave them there. I get down on the river and I've go no flies. I was stomping around all mad.

Anyway, Dick Zane used to give me some small flies that I would stick in my hat. He was a lousy tier. I thought, ah ha. I fished a dry line and caught more fish than I ever did before. That changed my thinking. It was unbelievable.

I watched a guy one day catch fish on a terrible-looking Skunk, it was all sog. I thought, I can't believe these fish would hit that. People think that fish are real smart but they're not. If I go through a run and get a tug I will always use a comeback pattern if I'm serious about catching him. We call it a pluck if you get that subtle tug.

A guy also needs to know about water temperature. If you feed fish in hatcheries 54-56 degrees is the best. That's when they are most aggressive. If it goes 48 they don't move as fast, they don't think as fast. If you go to 42 and you fish a sink-tip and you stick him you can come back in a few minutes because he doesn't remember very well. But if it's 56 and you stick him, oh man, you are not going to get him. If it goes 68, they close their mouths.

When you feed them in the hatchery at 48 you cut the feed in half and at 60 you cut the feed in half because they don't eat it. They go dormant both sides. Nelson's cut-off was 52 degrees and he would skate the flies. A degree or two makes a lot of difference to a fish and after years and years of catching them I used to just let them take it and hang on and hang on and they are not stuck and they will swing themselves right to shore. They'll hang right there and not until they turn does it stick them. They can feel the fly but they are not stuck so they go with it and they will lay right there.

The big argument around campfires is, why does the fish take? I've seen where I have made dozens of casts to a fish and after a while they will whack it, especially the younger fish that are more aggressive. I'm glad they do take but I don't think anybody really knows why.

I fish Muddlers and Bombers in the early season. I've had fish come 5-6 times for the fly. When they do that they will scare themselves. The fish scare themselves because the fish jumps and raises so much hell that they get scared.

After you catch hundreds and hundreds of them, (I've caught over 2,000 of them) you start experimenting and doing different things. When you fish behind people and it works you know that there is something different.

Spey Rods

This Spey stuff and twittering the fly at the end and the holographic materials, as far as I'm concerned there's something going on. I mostly fish two-handed rods anymore. After 30 years of single-handed casting you start to wear your arm out and the double-handed is so much easier, but it took me a long time to make the switch.

Jimmy Green has taught a lot of us and now we are as good as a lot of those guys from the Golden Gate casting club. Spey casting takes a while to learn. We designed our own fly lines to throw our sink-tips so they cast like a dry line.

Jimmy has taught us a lot about rods. When you build a graphite rod from scratch you learn. I've broken more rods than most people will ever own in their life by casting them. I hit them pretty hard. I have longer arms and it makes a difference. If there is anything wrong with a rod I'll find it real quick. I was always Jimmy's tester.

Ronde Story

One day the Ronde was muddy so we were fishing the mouth and that's when I came up with the spin and glow fly. It is lime green and bright fluorescent orange. I hooked into a big male at the top of the run and when he jumped I could see it was a big fish. Then he decided to leave the pool and he took off down river. I had a little bitty Sunbeam trout reel on and he run me out of line, so I would run down the river and I passed everybody clear down to the boat ramp at Beamers.

There was a guy putting in a boat and he says, what are we going to do, and I said stay right where you are, I was just about out of line and I went between his boat and the car and right on down through to the dead water below Beamers. It was a 20-plus-pound fish, a big male. I caught another one up there the same size.

That was a fun fish. I ran one mile down river with that little Sunbeam reel just screaming, right on empty. That is what it is all about.

It takes five years to start learning water. You also have to catch a lot of fish. Wherever you catch a fish there's a reason why's he's there. Then you put it all together and start figuring it out. The river holds many secrets. You're unlocking secrets every time you fish a river.

Best I ever did was 21 in one day. I've never done it since. The closest to it is probably 15 then 12. But it was awesome. My biggest fish was 22 poundss.

You never know when a big one will hit, it can take hours of fishing. I start fishing in September on the Ronde. You call around and keep in touch with guys to see if the fish are in. As soon as someone would hook one fish we knew they were there. October 1 there was always fish there. The wild fish always got there by October 1. The whole month of October was always good and then it would taper down.

A lot of guys hate strike indicators. When the river is blown out a lot of guys do it. I tried it a little this year because I had never done it before. I call it bobbing and jigging. It was fun learning. It's deadly. You can catch them underneath fast water.

Jimmy is right, there is no art involved. It's bobber fishing. The Canadians do it, they started it up there. They are using a corky on their fly line and it's deadly. It's the same thing as bobbing and jigging, it's deadly as hell. If people want to fish that way fine, I can't get down on them.

The only thing about that method is you don't get a take on the swing. The main thing for most of us in steelheading is the take. I'm kind of like Harry Lemire, after he's done fighting it he said, I wish I could just punch a button and straighten my hook out and let the fish go and then I wouldn't have to bring him in.

Elmer Crow

Elmer Crow is a Nez Perce tribal member who still exercises his treaty rights by dip netting for salmon on the Rapid River near Riggins, Idaho.

Elmer Crow is a respected Nez Perce elder and lifetime fisherman. He is a descendant of Chief Five Crow who was a half brother to Chief Joseph Sr. and is the only fly-fisherman that I know of who can legitimately claim the Clearwater as home. He was born near Orofino next to the Clearwater, as was his father.

He has fished the Clearwater since the 1940s and remembers fishing at the age of three. Elmer is one of the few tribal members who speak fluent Nez Perce. He has served the tribe as a member of the Game and Fish Commission and worked with other tribes and government agencies for several years as a participant of the Columbia River Inter-Tribal Fish Commission.

We have spent the morning talking fly-fishing and he has my undivided attention as he relates a fishing story passed down through his family's oral history. I have just told him about an account I have read recorded by Alexander Ross in 1813, an early Northwest explorer. Ross gives the account related below about some Nez Perce he observed fishing on the Snake River.

> On putting on shore to breakfast, four Indians on horseback joined us. The moment they alighted, one set about hobbling their horses, another to gather small sticks, a third to make a fire, and the fourth to catch fish. For this purpose, the fisherman cut off a bit of his leathern shirt, about the size of a small bean; then pulling out two or three horse hairs from his horse's tail for a line, tied the bit of leather to one end of it, in place of a hook or fly. Thus prepared, he entered the river a little way, sat down on a stone, and began throwing the small fish, three or four inches long, on shore, just as fast as he pleased; and while he was thus employed, another picked them up and threw them towards the fire, while the third stuck them up round it in a circle, on small sticks, and they were no sooner up than roasted. The fellows then sitting down, swallowed them, head, tails, bones, guts, fins, and all, in no time, just as one would swallow the yolk of an egg. Now all this was done before our man had his kettle ready for the fire, the Indians were already eating their breakfast. When the fish had hold of the bit of wet leather, or bait, their teeth got entangled in it, so as to give them time to jerk them on shore, which was to us a new mode of angling.

Elmer leans forward in his chair and says, "That's true, but you need to realize our people were fishing with sinew lines long before we had the horse. Sinew from deer and elk can be spun into long lengths. One of my uncles related a story to me when I was young. He told me that his grandfather had fished for steelhead and salmon with a willow rod, sinew line, and a bone hook with grouse feathers tied on it. They liked the grouse feathers because they were dark. They used chicken and grouse bones that were hollow and small. They weren't built like the hooks you see nowadays. They were kind of curly-qued with a little bit

Traditional Nez Perce salmon and steelhead fly, made from elk bone, elk sinew and feather. Fishing rods like the one in this photo were made from service berry.

of a hook on one side. They would catch steelhead with them where Lolo Creek flows into the Clearwater," he says.

Elmer Crow has just confirmed what I have suspected for a long time. The Nez Perce have not only been fishing for salmon and steelhead with spears and gaffs for thousands of years but they probably have been fly-fishing for at least two hundred years and maybe longer.

Elmer: Historically, there were two runs of steelhead, the larger fish would come in around August and seek out the deeper holes. Later on the smaller fish would arrive. The large fish would go all the way up to Kelly Creek and all the tributaries of the North Fork. Steelhead spawned in all of those streams. The Dworshak hatchery started their original brood stock from those

Elmer Crow not only used the Woolly Bugger to catch trout but also used it to catch many steelhead.

Black Woolly Bugger
(tied by Dave Clark)

Tail: Black marabou
Body: Black chenille
Hackle: Black, palmered

Kelly Creek fish. They were some of the biggest steelhead in the country. Those big fish also ran up the Lochsa and its tributaries as well as the Selway and Meadow Creek.

I think I am one of the few people that have actually caught steelhead on a fly in the North Fork and on Kelly Creek and Moose Creek. You could look in those pools on Kelly Creek, and see steelhead up to 30 pounds that looked like logs laying on the bottom. In those days, we went up there for a couple of weeks to hunt and fish. We smoked and dried the fish to use later in the winter. We would bring back the fish and game and give it to a lot of the tribal members who were unable to provide for themselves.

I caught my first steelhead in Kelly Creek in 1959 on a bumble bee pattern in the subsurface with a one-piece bamboo rod. What I would do was to make a cast and then let the fly float down river by letting the line slide through my fingers. I didn't have a reel or any backing and I just wrapped the line around my hand.

My dad taught me how to fly-fish when I was small and I think dad was probably one of the first modern day fly-fishermen on the Clearwater. To my best recollection, dad was catching steelhead on a fly in 1951. He taught me and I ended

This traditional Nez Perce elk bone and feather caught a steelhead in the Clearwater River.

up fly-fishing the North Fork country close to where Kelly Creek Ranger Station is now located.

Dad was a self-taught fly-fisherman that became interested in the sport by reading *Field & Stream* magazines in the late 1940s and early 1950s. I couldn't read at the time but I remember looking at the pictures. Dad sent away for one of the fly rods that were advertised in that magazine. In 1951 dad bought his first fly tying kit from Snyder's sporting goods store in Orofino on Johnson Avenue. Dad taught himself to tie flies and to cast from reading the magazine.

We used sinking lines and wet flies. Dad used variations of the traditional salmon flies and preferred patterns with white wings that moved when the current hit them. I have made some modifications to that fly but have never divulged how it was made. I let it flow in the current and strip it a little to make the wings move and sometimes those steelhead go crazy. I fish it a few inches under the water. A lot of times those fish will hit that fly on the retrieve.

Another favorite pattern was a large gray mayfly but I don't remember what it looked like exactly. It was about twice the size of a normal mayfly. I also fished with black and chartreuse Woolly Buggers and bright-colored streamers. I normally don't fish when the fish are moving but I like to fish holding water that I have discovered over the years. I started using a floating line in the late 1960s.

My first Clearwater steelhead was caught near Greer in the late 1950s. I caught it on a big mayfly. I remember in the 1960s seeing some of those California fishermen and what stands out in my mind was the quality and quantity of their equipment. They had beautiful rods and reels, and they had tackle we never even thought of. I asked them one time what their rods cost and I couldn't believe that anyone would pay $78 for a rod.

When I don't care whether or not I land a fish I use a 7 1/2-foot 5-weight trout rod with 6-pound-test line. The reason I do that is because I enjoy the bite, that's what I really enjoy. That's what fishing is, you have to hoodwink the animal into biting and I believe they deserve an extra chance to get away, so I use light gear. Sometimes they will come up with an open mouth and the

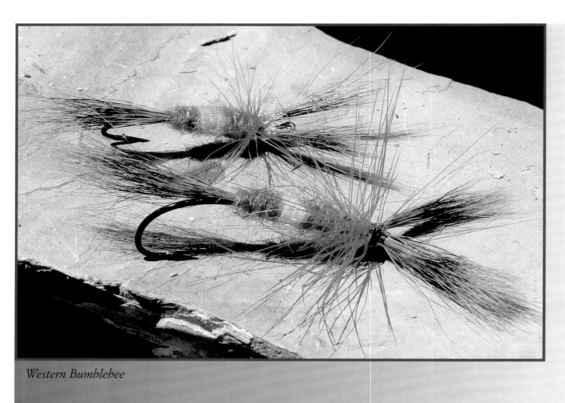

Western Bumblebee

Bumblebee
(tied by Dave Clark)

Tail: Squirrel tail
Body: Orange or yellow
    and brown wool
Hackle: Red
Antennae: Squirrel tail

fly and the water will rush in. You have to have the discipline not to jerk the fly at that time, you can't put any pressure on them until they turn and start that first run.

One of my most memorable steelhead was a 17-pounder in 1963 in Whiskey Creek in Orofino when I was fly-fishing for trout. I had a cheap trout rod, and was fishing with a #12 Black Gnat. I was 23 years old, and recently married. Me and my dog were fishing, my wife dropped us off and I was going to fish about a mile back to the house. I was just going to catch a mess of trout for supper.

It was about noon and me and my dog were getting hungry so I got a sandwich out of my backpack and started to eat. I flipped the fly out on the water just for the heck of it and kept on eating. It wasn't long before the fly sank and the line went tight and I thought I was snagged up, then a funny thought came to me, I probably have a great big steelhead on so I grabbed the rod and jerked it and down the creek the line went. I had to run like a son of a gun to catch up and one hour and 20 minutes later I landed a 17-pound fish. I hadn't fly-fished for a while and had started again and I had just bought that trout rod, it was a cheap $2.98 fly rod, it was a 4 piece bamboo and I had an $8 fly reel and a $7 dollar line and an 8-pound-test leader.

The biggest steelhead I ever saw on the Clearwater was caught by my 7-year-old son Jared in 1972 near Little Myrtle and it tipped the scales at the Lapwai general store at exactly 32 pounds. It was 47 inches long and would have been a state record at the time, but the state wouldn't recognize it because the season was still closed to white guys on the Clearwater. Since the fishing season was closed to whites they wouldn't officially recognize it as a record. The state only counted records during the officially recognized season.

In the early years I hooked several 40-plus-inch fish on a fly but did not land very many of them. Most of them came loose

Elmer Crow caught a steelhead on Kelly Creek with this pattern in the early 1950s. He is one of a very few who caught steelhead in the stream.

right next to the bank. I never felt bad about losing them because that animal had given me a lot of enjoyment up to that point, so why shouldn't it go free?

When I'm fishing it's a time of remembrance of past days fishing with my father. I have a son that is a fly-fisherman and it makes me thrill to realize that this is something that carries on, that these fish have been put here to be taken and we do take them but they are also meant to be enjoyed. I do the same thing with my son that my father did with me and we spend time on the river every year trying to catch those steelhead. It's something that binds each generation together and it brings back a lot of memories about experiences with my family and my brother the fish.

Thorson Bennett fished the Grande Ronde and throughout the Pacific Northwest in the 1950s.

Thorson Bennett

Thorson is quoted as saying: "My grandfather settled Enterprise, Oregon, and my dad was born there in 1874. I was delivered to him at Elgin in 1903, not far from the banks of my favorite river (Grande Ronde), which I've fished most of a lifetime."

He graduated high school from Milton Freewater, attended college at Whitworth in Spokane and got a Master's degree at Washington State University. He first taught school at Parma, Idaho in the 1920s and then went to Bear Creek and Laurel, Montana where he coached and taught the sciences.

His daughter Nancy doesn't think Thorson started fishing the Ronde till after 1946 and probably not until the late 50s or early 60s. That's when the family moved from Montana to Kennewick, Washington where he became a high school principal. He corresponded a lot with Ted Trueblood and his daughter thinks he may have found out about the Ronde from him.

For many years, he would take a motor home and camp at the mouth of the Ronde. His wife Beth also fly-fished for steelhead. They would enter accuracy casting contests in Kennewick and many times she would do better than Thorson, which usually didn't sit very well with him, but his daughter said he really enjoyed telling others how good a fly-caster Beth was.

Walt Price, Jr. recalled in an article that he wrote for *The Creel* in 1976, that Thorson was a striking man, tall and lean. His bony frame was topped with a long, angular stance and a full head of wild hair. Rick Miller said that when Thorson was out in the river all alone he reminded him of a great blue heron.

Grande Ronde Story
by Thorson Bennett (October 9, 1968)

Yagers Regret

I had fished fruitlessly through a beautiful bright calm but chilly yesterday without being disturbed by any other fishermen. I was planning another peaceful and leisurely day, so I was in not hurry to get down to the river. After a good breakfast I heard a car pull off the road.

I opened the door or the camper and saw a man and woman assembling their tackle.

"Why aren't you fishing?" he asked me.

I replied, "The water is not right. Yesterday's rain and the cold night have lowered the water temperature more than the steelhead like."

"Oh, well," he said, "I'm looking for salmon, not steelhead."

I noticed the large night crawlers dangling from the pair of single hooks on his spinning gear. "What will you do if a steelhead takes one of those," I asked. "Will you keep it?"

He grinned sheepishly but had no reply.

The Chappie and its variations was Thorson Bennett's favorite pattern. The fly shown here was actually fished by Thorson.

Chappie

(tied by Thorson Bennett, this fly was used by Thorson)

Tail: Golden pheasant tippets

Head: Orange.

Tail: Tips of town long and narrow Plymouth Rock hackles. The hackles are as long as the body dressed on a regular hook and may be placed back to back if desired.

Body: Orange wool, medium thick.

Ribbing: Orange silk thread. Throat: Two or three turns of a Plymouth Rock hackle tied on as a collar and not tied downward. The throat is sparse but as long as the body.

Wing: The tips of two long and narrow Plymouth Rock hackles. The wing extends nearly to the end of the tail and is dressed very high on the hook. The hackles may be placed back to back if desired. "Outdoor" Franklin preferred a Mustad #3906 regular-shank hook.

How Not to Wade the Grande Ronde
by Thorson Bennett

So much has been written on the subject of how to wade a stream without going under that there is little I can add, but no one has ever told how wading shouldn't be done.

Beth and I had made a late start from Kennewick to reach the Grande Ronde some 200 miles away, and when we arrived the light was almost gone from the evening's fishing.

Everyone knows the usual ritual which a fly-fisherman must perform before he approaches the stream. Well you know how long it takes a woman to change her wardrobe for any occasion and since I wanted Beth to have an even start with me, I assembled her equipment knowing she had other more important things to look after.

As I laid out her waders and non-skid sandals I warned her about the slippery ledge as one entered the stream. I didn't take much time getting ready with waders and started towards the river carrying my felt-soled sandals which I planned to put on at stream side. As I went down the hill I saw Beth in the water below me and I saw that she had dropped her fly book in the water and it was floating down stream.

This stimulated me to action, so down I charged to retrieve the flies and forgetting that I did not have on the non-skid shoes I charged out onto the slippery shelf and disappeared under the water. Beth screamed, "Thorson!"

The only proof that I had entered the water was my hat which floated downstream behind the fly book. As I reappeared Beth was standing up to her knees in the riffle below awaiting the flies and hat. Needless to say, it was a barren evening since my immersion had sent all the fish back to the sea.

The Creel Article
by Walt Price

Much of the information about Thorson provided below was taken with permission by Robert Wethern from the January 1976 edition of *The Creel* that was written by Walt Price. Walt Price is the one who first started using the greased-line technique on the Ronde in the early 60s.

Walt: I recall that Thorson liked to fish the Ronde the most the last of October and November. Possibly his preference for this time of year was due to the reduction of fishermen and the solitude we all enjoy but so seldom find in this day and age."

He liked to use "large flies, hackles of gray and brown and wings of squirrel, fox, deer, and bear hair. They were enormous, especially compared to the sparse greased-line flies I gave him."

Wes Drain recalls that, "The last time I saw Thorson he was on the Ronde. I think the year before my little adventure on the Snake. He was carrying that huge, yellow fiberglass rod of his and had his old faithful Chappie fly on."

Thorson had an understandable dislike and mistrust, initially, for all invaders of his beloved boyhood river, especially bait and hardware slingers. Normally he was slow to speak and even when so moved he interspersed many silent stares into the hills between his conversational comments.

However, when a car pulled up alongside our "talk sessions," he would be the first to answer the intruder: "Naw! Fishing's real slow .... the Ronde's not what it used to be, you know!" Whenever Thorson went into that routine, we would look out over the river to the hills, ourselves, as if to escape.

He fished equally well with right or left hand and once, borrowing my rod, tried to teach me to do so. He revealed the up or downstream mends one could throw, of line delivery, with either hand. And, he was adept at mending the line without disturbing the fly's drift.

One day he followed me along the bank of the river and I noticed he was winding all the monofilament he could find around a fairly large rock. Finally, it got to me and I asked, 'Thorson, what the hell are you going to do with all that line?"

He hefted the rock and responded, "Oh, it keeps me busy, when I don't have anything else to do. So, I make sure the bait boys have something to catch." With that, threw the rock, with its bird's nest of monofilament, plunk, into a Grande Ronde drift favored by bait fishermen!

As interested as he genuinely seemed in our greased-line technique, he invariably fished a large, full-dressed fly. His glass rods were long, with large-diameter butts. His fly lines were sinkers or sink-tips. He never did cast a long line.

Thorson once fished our style, and it was the one and only time he fished with us. We picked him up at his camp one evening for a change-of-pace try in the Snake, and I put him into a small pocket at the head of a long run, just around the corner from the confluence of the Ronde.

It was an exciting time for anglers who wade deep, the quiet strength of the vast water filling us with awe. The shadows were long, from steep canyon walls, and a warm wind blew upstream, rendering every line mend to perfection. The same soft wind carried waves of small caddis, which coated our windward sides and crawled in and out of our ears.

The hour then was so magic that I still remember it as if it only now were happening ....

....the whitefish are on a feeding spree and small bass jump clear of the water with a burring sound of their tails. Our fish are here, too, and one comes, rolling and humping the water before it. My fly is pulled hard and I have missed a nice fish, far out, at the peak of my cast ....

....below me, Jerry Larson is into a nice fish. It throws water and runs, far into the middle of the Snake. Jerry Boeder busts a fish off setting the hook. We three are busting with conversation now, when I turn toward Thorson. Quietly, he has worked a steelhead into shallow water. I wade to Thorson and beach a nice hen fish for him. In the corner of its mouth, I note, is a small, greased-line fly I had given Thorson years back. It was his compliment to me. Filled with emotion, I looked up at him and quietly said to myself, "Thank you, Thorson!"

By all accounts, one of Thorson's favorite patterns that he used almost exclusively on the Ronde was the Chappie fly. The original pattern is credited to C.L. "Outdoor" Franklin who was an outstanding fly tier. The dressing was described in November 1949 issue of *Field & Stream,* and the following year in the book, *Streamer Fly-fishing,* by Joseph D. Bates, Jr.

Snake River near Asotin, Washington.

1960s

Ted Trueblood

Ted Trueblood was the symbol of the true American sportsman and was an outdoor editor for *Field & Stream* for several years. Trueblood's hunting and fishing articles inspired many an outdoorsman for many years. His long-time friend Peter Barrett wrote an article about Trueblood in 1970 and said he was an excellent hunter and fisherman, but above all he was a conservationist. He was a good camp cook, a philosopher, writer, and outdoorsman.

He wrote hundreds of short articles about the outdoors and authored two books entitled, *The Angler's Handbook* (1949) and *The Hunter's Handbook* (1954). He grew up in Homedale, Idaho near the Snake River and fished that river at an early age. His grandfather bought him a bamboo fly rod when he graduated from high school and he bought his own shotgun at the age of thirteen.

He was a long-time member of Ducks Unlimited and the Wildlife Federation and was one of the movers behind getting

Ted Trueblood wrote the first steelhead article in True *magazine about the Grande Ronde River in the early 1960s and called it the "unnamed river". Photo by Jim Green.*

the Frank Church River of No Return designated as a wilderness area. He was also one of the first writers in the 1960s to warn the general public about the negative effects that dams would have on salmon and steelhead on the Columbia and Snake rivers.

He was a good friend of Bill Schaadt and fished with him and others including Mel Leven, Jimmy Green, and Duke Parkening on the Russian and Eel rivers for salmon and steelhead in Northern California.

Ted Trueblood probably first fly-fished for steelhead on the Grande Ronde in 1960 and wrote the first article about any of the local rivers in *True Magazine* in 1961, entitled, "I Found Steelhead Shangri-la." He says in the article that the river is known for its winter-run fish but he may be one of the first who caught summer-run fish and says that when he and Clare Conley fished it that they had no competition. That article also included photos that introduced the general public to the area for the first time.

In that article and succeeding articles he referred to the Ronde as the unnamed river. He indicates that the locals fished the river in the winter, but thought that very few people knew that there were summer fish also. The article doesn't indicate what time of the year he fished it. He could actually have been fishing for winter fish that were early arrivals. He caught his first fish on a Fall Favorite after first trying a Thor and a Black Prince.

The Black Gordon was one of the first flies used by Ted Trueblood on the Grande Ronde.

Black Gordon
(tied by Dave Clark)

Body: 1/3 red, 2/3 black with gold ribbing
Wing: Black or dark bucktail

He wrote another story about fly-fishing for steelhead on the Ronde in *Field & Stream* in 1963 but still called it the unnamed river. He fished it in October with Ed Ward who was married to actress Jane Wyatt.

On that trip he fished with a sinking line and started out with a Fall Favorite, switched to a Gregory's Black Bug, then to a dark Klamath River fly and got his first strike on a #6 Bucktail Royal Coachman. That first wild fish weighed five pounds. A short time later, Ed Ward caught his first fish on a #8 Black Gordon.

After that first fish, Ted switched to a #8 Black Fairy which was a lightly dressed Atlantic salmon pattern. In the next couple of hours he hooked several fish with that fly.

In the article there is an incident that bears repeating. At the end of the day a violent wind storm came through that made it impossible to fish. They gave up and went back to camp to eat a sandwich. By the time they finished eating, the wind had stopped and they noticed dozens of rising fish in the pool they had been fishing. They didn't think they could be steelhead because there were so many, and besides it looked like these were feeding fish.

Trueblood said, "My curiosity became more and more insistent. The rises were quiet and businesslike, such as those made by big brown trout when they are seriously working a hatch. I walked down to the water's edge to try to learn what these boisterous fish were taking. When I got close enough to see, I discovered that the wind had blown in thousands of grasshoppers. The water was peppered with them. The fish, whatever they were, obviously were taking grasshoppers.

"It was too much; I had to know what they were. Hurriedly I changed my sinking line to a floating one and tied on a grasshopper dry fly. A fish rose thirty feet away. I cast to him. He took the fly. I missed him. Another engulfed the hopper a few feet farther out. He came willingly to my fly, and I missed him too.

"I was striking too fast. When the third fish hit and my fly disappeared, I raised the tip deliberately and I was in to a solid fish. A fraction of a second later, I knew what I had: A steelhead about 6 or 7 pounds shot into the air.

This was a great moment. For years I had been trying to take steelhead on a dry fly, but I'd never succeeded. Now I actually had one on and I could still see a dozen more rising whenever I glanced up or down the pool.

"I caught three more before it got too dark to fish a floating fly. Of course, I missed several and lost others, but I always lose some steelhead fly-fishing. I may have caught more staying with a conventional wet fly, but I was happy and was perfectly content with the dry fly. The entire afternoon and evening had been great."

At the end of the article he left the following advice for all would-be steelhead fly-fishermen. "The most important thing of all," he says, "is to fish hard and keep moving. The more stream you cover, the better your chances, and the man who has his fly in the water ten hours a day will inevitably catch more than another who sits on the bank and talks. As the tomcat said, 'If you want to do business, you've got to make calls!'"

Trueblood never did divulge the name of the Grande Ronde River in any of his articles. He made at least one film documentary on the river fly-fishing for steelhead, but again the name of the river was not given. Trueblood introduced fishermen such as Ed Ward, Clare Conley, Mel Leven and Jim and Carol Green to the Ronde in the 1960s. He fished with Jim Green every fall on the Ronde and elsewhere for several years.

Walt (Dub) Price

Walt Price is the fisherman that is given credit for introducing the grease lining technique on the Grande Ronde in the early 1960s.

By all accounts Walt (Dub) Price is given credit for introducing grease lining to this area in the early 1960s on the Grande Ronde. Walt was an artist from Seattle and a member of the Everett fly-fishing fraternity. Bill Nelson and others told him about the Ronde and he fished the it for a few years starting in the early 60s. Sometimes he would come over in a small trailer with his wife and camp with the Nelson gang.

Walt taught Bill Nelson and his group how to grease line and also taught Bob Weddell who in turn passed this knowledge on to Glen Brackett, Duke Parkening and Keith Stonebraker. Walt attended Humboldt State College in the 1950s where he became friends with Jim Adams and Glen Brackett. Bob Weddell also attended Humboldt State and was one of the reasons they got along so well when they met on the Ronde in 1967.

The following article about grease lining written by Walt in 1967 in the April issue of "The Creel" and was reprinted with permission by Robert Wethern.

Up and Over, Easy Does It

It was four years ago last September that Bill Nelson and I slipped away from camp while my wife slept and Lew Bell and Dick Denman poked weary eyes at us from a tent flap. This was a small ritual for Bill and me-each morning we would fish a few new spots before breakfast, and it gave us a chance to talk of old times and try out new ideas. This proved to be a morning that would change my whole outlook on steelhead angling.

Bill had led me to a rough, pocket-filled stretch of water, and he cut its inky blackness with a new high-density sinking line. After about 20 minutes, he turned and said, "Not here this morning, Dubber, you call the next shot." "Nope, you," I replied and handed him my outfit. Bill pulled line from the reel and started his false cast. He was a little awkward at first because of the unfamiliar feel of a double-tapered floating line and light rod in his hand.

Grasshopper
(tied by Dave Clark)
Tail: Red hackle fibers
Body: Yellow with palmered light brown hackle
Wing: Turkey
Head and collar: Deer hair

Walt Price loved to dry-fly fish for steelhead and grasshoppers were among his favorite patterns.

"Keep it short, Bill," I said, "Hold it where you want it by mending the line."

On about the third cast a beautiful hump broke the oily slick, the broad back rolling out and over, and the almost eerie wiggle of the dorsal fin showing. Then the wet line was slapping and stinging our faces. "Did you see that?" Bill sucked in a few bugs, and I let out my whoop.

It was like a dream come true. The next four fish cinched it, rolling up and over like choice rainbows on a feeding spree, only lazy, clean and deliberate. Bill settled down and struck the fifth one hard. After a long, hard run through the heavy water he broke the hook of the small fly. We were like two kids all the way back to camp.

One day later Lew Bell scrambled from the water, hastily ran a floating line through the rod guides and thrashed his way back into the river. We did not see him until after dark, and when he reported in he said, "Hells bells, Dub, this is just glorified trout fishing . . . I'm a happy man again. Never did care for all this heavy gear."

What was this new-found secret? No secret at all. Just a simple adaptation of grease-line fishing originated a long time ago for taking Atlantic salmon. I can assure you that the application of the technique and theory of fishing the fly in various sizes in and just below the surface film is dynamite for steelhead at certain times. Using the floating line as a controlling agent, you will find that you will be more efficient in water coverage. You can hold or delay your fly where you wish. You can drift it free and void of any drag. For the first time you will be able to see just where your fly lies, what it is doing, and what you can do with it by mending your floating line.

When you move a fish you will know it. He will either show himself or your visible line will tell you the story. If conditions are not correct for him, the fish will do several movements. He will, of course, turn abruptly away from the fly, bulging the water. He may actually porpoise directly over your fly or hit it with his side or tail.

I once had a fish strike my fly no less than seven times with its side and tail. I kept trying to come back on my line but felt nothing each time. Finally, when my fly reached the pocket again, instead of stopping it, I allowed the fly to continue its drift. The fish came again, rolled and ever so slightly the line slowed, turned down and I felt a gentle pull. I merely had to tighten the line and there he was.

The secret is the natural float or the use of slight or natural drag that still allows your fly to have life to its movements in the river currents. When everything is proper, the fish will come slowly and deliberately, take your fly and return to his lie. Now you have actually seen the fish or the bulge of water that marked his position. He has definitely moved to your fly.

You can strike now and take your chances or you can turn your attention to your line. The line will begin to belly or pull down. Invariably, you will now feel the fish. Now you strike. It is not necessary to tumble him in the current. If the delay is proper he will feel the strike from the side or from behind. The fish will move forward and help you even more. Many times a fish has taken my fly in a chop or heavy water. The immediate line belly told me of the take, and the current and start of the fish set the hook. Before I could move, I was into a running fish, soundly hooked.

I am not an advocate of a clean perfect drift at all times to your fly. In fact I find myself more and more delaying my fly or slowing it down over productive lies as I cover the water. To do this one must halt the natural drift. As long as the fly continues to convey movement and life you are still in the game.

If your fly is dragging too fast, you may move a good fish who wants it badly, but when he strikes, the fish will bust the water wide open, scare you half to death, and bounce your slackened line hard. What has happened is that he has rushed the fly and in taking it has turned away abruptly. The moving line simply pulled the fly from his mouth. You will not be quick enough to hit such a fish.

Without a doubt, I carry too many flies for practical purposes, but I enjoy experimenting with a wild assortment of patterns. I think it is wiser to carry various sizes and shapes rather than one or two sizes in various colors. I have found the dark patterns, especially black, to be extremely effective. Flies should not be dressed too heavily. Rather, build into your creation materials that will be supple and will convey life in the current; and not stiff or broom like. A bushy fly is quite often fished with the idea that it is easier to see. If conditions are right, fish can see the fly no matter how small it is. When you have a good fish take in heavy water with a wisp of hackle and wing on a small hook you will know what I am talking about.

I do not believe steelhead are too selective in their choice of fly pattern. However, I do believe they are extremely sensitive to how the fly is presented to them. By all means fish a fly in which you have confidence, and utilize its various sizes throughout the day. Change sizes to match the water, and change your tippet weight to match the fly. A tiny fly will not fish effectively in heavy water, and a larger fly will not produce lifelike movement in slow water.

I cannot yet say just when one should turn from deep fly to grease line with regard to water temperatures. My only experience has been with summer fish, so warm water temperatures existed already. My experiments with cold-water winter fish have been failures so far. However, I have found a remarkable difference in the response to grease-line fishing in accordance with the environmental conditioning of the fish. This seems to be an all-important factor.

I have had very little luck in our streams west of the Cascades as compared to the eastern side. The Snake, Grand Ronde, and Columbia rivers have been excellent. Yet, my beloved Stillaguamish and Skykomish rivers, under the same water temperatures and conditions, have been low in fish response.

It seems the longer the fish run in fresh water the more responsive they become. The adjustment of the fish to his environment is therefore enhanced by the length of the river it must run. A fall fish sucking in your fly in the Snake or Columbia System has been in fresh water for several months, or perhaps since spring. If you should be casting in the riffle below Deer Creek on the Stillaguamish it is not inconceivable that you are over fish that entered the river no more than two days before. I know those fish are slower to respond.

If water clarity, temperature, and environmental conditions are adequate you will take more fish with the grease line than any other method. This does not mean that you will not continue to take fish with a sunken fly under the same conditions, or the spoon or bait boys will not continue to take their share. However, with the grease line it will be a bonanza!

Last year on the Grand Ronde, my partner and I were two days into our trip and fishless. It was apparent that we were too early. On the third day, late in the evening, we sat, disgruntled, high on the flood bed of the Snake River. Looking down on this vast movement of water we watched perhaps 10 or 12 spin anglers spread out along the gravel bar.

Since early that morning six fish had been killed and two lost. Four of these fish were the limits of two anglers who were just leaving. Two others had killed a fish each and one also lost a fish. A fifth angler lost his fish. So, during the day's rotation, there had been 15 anglers in this piece of water with an average of four hours fishing time each. What do we have? Fifteen fishermen with 60 hours total fishing time and only five of whom were involved with hooking the eight fish.

Jerry and I decided to give it a try and found we could wade out a little at the upper end of the beach. In approximately one and one-half hours we hooked and played on the reel 10 fish and perhaps moved two other fish. This episode and many other enjoyable hours spent with the grease line have only further proven to me the effectiveness of this technique. I can only say to other fly-fishermen—give it a try. It is worth the effort.

The North Fork of the Clearwater River was once the destination of large steelhead known as B-runs.

Duke Parkening

Chris (right) and Duke Parkening with a Clearwater steelhead taken in the early 1970s.

Duke is one of the original members of the Disney crowd that started fly-fishing the Clearwater for steelhead in the early 1960s. He was friends with Milt Kahl, Ed Ward, Mel Leven, Ken Petersen, and Ken Anderson who all worked as animators at the Walt Disney studio in California. Duke and his wife Betty moved from California to Idaho in 1969 and built a home on the Middle Fork of the Clearwater above Kamiah.

In California, Duke and his family were members of the Long Beach Casting Club and they both competed in flycasting tournaments. In California they became friends of Jim and Carol Green, Ted Trueblood, and others. Duke met Bob Weddell briefly on the Eel River one year and a few years later both men had moved permanently to this area.

Duke: Ken Anderson had fished the Clearwater in 1962 with Ted Trueblood and Eddy Ward and that was all Ken could talk about for a whole year. Ted and Ed were good friends of ours. Eddy Ward was married to actress Jane Wyatt. Ed and Jane would camp in the Lenore area and also on the Grande Ronde. I first fished the Clearwater in 1963 with Ken Petersen and then moved to the area in 1969.

I had first met these Disney guys at Hat Creek Ranch in California fly-fishing for trout. These guys started telling me about the Clearwater steelhead. Ken Andersen was delirious and enraptured with the Clearwater. I decided to learn how to steelhead fish and first started fishing for steelhead on the Klamath and the Trinity. Those fish were called half-pounders but most were 5-6 pounds. If you got a 12-pound fish on the Klamath, that was a big fish.

Ken Anderson, Ken Petersen and myself would have lunch together once a week. I would drive over to Burbank and we would have lunch in the commissary and many times Walt Disney would be there. Do you know what we would talk about? We talked about the Clearwater River. That was all we talked about, we were consumed about this fantastic place up here.

I caught a 14-pound fish on the Trinity one year and the newspaper came out and took a picture of me because it was such a large fish. That was nothing compared to the Clearwater fish. Those were large fish and all wild, we couldn't sleep nights when we came over here and stayed in motels in Clarkston. We would get up in the middle of the night and start talking about the fabulous fishing. It was unbelievable.

You know it's kind of a shame that we pay so much attention to flies, rods, reels, lines and all that other equipment that we are supposed to have. All that stuff is meaningless if we don't have a fishery. Why is it that we can afford to spend time and money on equipment but as a society won't make the necessary effort to save the resource? The majority of the people who like to fish for

Duke Parkening brought the Copper Colonel with him from California and used it to catch a lot of steelhead on the Clearwater River.

Copper Colonel
(tied by Dave Clark)

Body: Any material with a copper look
Wing: Black Bucktail

steelhead and salmon will never actually get involved in an organization or donate money to help fish-restoration efforts. Very few people will ever attend a public meeting and make their feelings known.

My favorite patterns would have to include the Black Skunk or Special Skunk, Copper Colonel, Golden Demon, Purple Peril and Skykomish Sunrise. These are the patterns I used on the Klamath and Trinity when I first started to fly-fish for steelhead. The Copper Colonel is my favorite fly on the Clearwater. I think the pattern may have originated with Cal Bird who was a friend of mine.

My techniques changed when I met Bob Weddell who lives in Orofino. Bob educated me to the Purple Peril and showed me that Clearwater steelhead could be caught using the greased-line technique. We fished below Riverside one time and the two of us together took 29 fish in two days all on that one fly, all greased line, all floating line.

Bob introduced me to that fly and to fishing strictly top water. Up until that time I used a lot of Wet Cell lines and shooting heads that sank, but Bob was fishing a dry line with a wet fly. Shortly after that, Keith Stonebraker started using surface flies with riffle hitches, I think Bob had something to do with that too.

We were here when Dworshak was going in and when they were putting in that diversion tunnel. I couldn't believe it was being built. We had the most unbelievable steelhead fishing that you could ever imagine, can you imagine hooking 55 fish in six days and fish weighing up to 21 pounds? We had fish on all day long, all caught on flies, and we released all of them. It was the reason I came up here, I couldn't think of anything but the Clearwater after that first trip.

I fished the North Fork before Dworshak with Perk Lyda from Orofino. Perk had a guiding business out of Orofino. He has picture after picture of 20-pound fish from that area. The North Fork was the real wild and scenic river, the most pristine of them all.

Dworshak started affecting the fishing long before it was completed. My son Chris and I came up here in 1966 and had some fabulous fishing for six days. On our last day we were on our way home and we saw Ed Ward and Milt Kahl. We stopped to talk for a while and then went back to California. I talked to Ed later and he informed me that the fishing had been terrible. The Corp was working on the diversion tunnel and the water below Orofino was chocolate brown for several days.

The dams have created such a different environment, that the timing of the fish runs has been thrown off. I've heard stories about fish going over the dams twice because they get disoriented. The whole system has been completely screwed up. We used to have a saying in the real estate business, if you sell a guy something good you never hear from him again, but if you sell him something bad, you have him for life because he will try to trade it on motels or trust deeds or boats or anything to get out of the deal.

That's what the Corp has done to us, they've traded us peanuts for diamonds. Now they are telling us that they are going to fix it but it continues to be a political mess and Bush is not coming through. He knew zero about steelhead and salmon and dams, but yet he told us that we are going to save the dams as well as the fish.

I have been told by people that taking out the earthen portion of those dams is no more than a three-day job and one of the arguments is that the silt could become a big problem, yet now there is a proposed action to dredge 106 miles of the Columbia three feet deep, what about the silt problems related to that operation?

Tom Morgan

Tom Morgan lived in Clarkston, Washington where he fished with Bob Weddell and Keith Stonebraker.

Tom is one of the local characters that no longer resides in the area. He lived in Clarkston, Washington in the late 1960s and was an avid steelhead fly-fisherman. Keith Stonebraker was his first mentor, but he also spent a lot of time fishing with Bob Weddell and Glen Brackett. He presently lives in Montana where he keeps busy inventing and marketing bamboo rod tools and fly rods under the name of his new company, Tom Morgan Rodsmiths.

What many people may not know is that Tom has been paralyzed by multiple sclerosis since 1995. He now is confined to a high-tech wheelchair and uses a voice-activated computer to help him talk. Those who know Tom will tell you that they have never heard him complain and he is an inspiration to all with whom he comes in contact. Most of Tom's inventions have come since he has been wheelchair bound.

People who have fished with him say he was a phenomenal caster and had excellent eyesight. In his own words, "I'm sure glad that I got in on the early days of fly-fishing with floating lines. Happily, I've never caught a steelhead on a sinking line although I came close."

Some of the information below, reprinted with Tom's permission, was taken from two previous interviews that Tom conducted with Bob Maulucci and a Japanese magazine.

Tom: I grew up on a motel at Ennis, Montana, and the home of the famous Madison River, and the not-so-famous O'Dell Creek and Spring Creek. It was more of a fishing resort than it was just a motel and many customers would spend vacations fishing. My first experiences with fly-fishing were with some of the customers that came to the motel. In the beginning I was a spin fisherman, and as a kid I fished mostly in Bear Creek that ran right through the motel grounds.

There were two motel customers that kept telling me that I should learn to fly-fish because it was more fun and could be even more productive than lure or bait fishing. Tom Coxon and Howard Sykes became my fly-fishing mentors. Tom lived in Florida at the time, but had been a stockbroker in New York City and grew up fishing in the Catskills. Howard lived in New Jersey, but had fished all over the world.

Both of them were accomplished fly-fishermen. They both used Leonard and Payne rods so I could see what those rods did for them. They got me started and for several years would let me go along with them and helped me learn the nuances of fly-fishing.

I moved to Clarkston in 1969 and lived there for about two years, but prior to that time I had fly-fished for steelhead on the Clearwater and Snake in 1964-65. I had fished with Keith Stonebraker and Doug Venerka on several occasions and we never caught a fish.

I met Bob Weddell in 66-67. Bob was a friend of Keith's and had introduced Keith and others to the greased-line technique that Bob had learned from Walt Price on the Grande Ronde. In the beginning I used either full-sinking lines or sink-tips. The patterns that I remember using the most then were the Fall Favorite and Green Butt Skunk. I fished for almost a month at different times over several years and never caught a steelhead. That seems hard to believe now with all of the wild fish that were around then, but it's true.

In looking back at it I just have to say that it was sheer stupidity. At that time we were told you had to have sinking lines and fish on the bottom. I had guided a lot of fishermen in Montana who had also fished for steelhead and they frankly put me on the wrong road. They told me that you had to know exactly where they were laying and you had to get the fly right next to them. I found out after fishing for steelhead that that isn't necessarily true.

I became acquainted with Bob Weddell through Keith Stonebraker just after Bob had talked with Dub Price at the mouth of the Grande Ronde. Dub had related to Bob how three of them had caught around 250 steelhead over a week's time fishing right around the mouth in the Snake. Neither of us could believe it. They were using a fly that, I believe, was called the Purple Peril. It had a purple body, mallard flank feathers, and dark soft hen feathers similar to a Spey fly only the feathers were shorter. They were fishing these flies using the greased-line method where you cast out at an approximate 45-degree angle, then put a mend in the line.

First Fish on Ronde

I tied some of these flies and headed to the Grande Ronde above Bogan's. I drove along until I spotted what I thought was a good run with the right speed and good rock cover on the bottom. I still didn't know much about what constituted a good steelhead run, but this looked like it would be a good trout run and I assumed they were the same.

I started working down the run and had only made a few casts when a steelhead started jumping near the middle of the river. I will never forget that it jumped nine times clear of the water.

That seemed amazing to me. I made another cast and realized that my Purple Peril was no longer on my line. The steelhead had taken the fly and I didn't even know it! That was really unusual because that was my first run, I had just tied on the fly very

carefully, and I felt nothing. I fished the rest of the day with no success. That was the first steelhead that I know that I hooked.

I used the Purple Peril for a lot of my fishing. Then I started to tie a very sparse Comet without any bead eyes. I used yellow and orange hackle on the head taking two wraps of each. It had a gold tinsel body and yellow and orange tail. As I say, this fly was very sparse. I usually tied it on a Mustad 9672 in sizes 6 and 8. This is the fly that I used most of the time on the Clearwater and Snake until I started dry-fly-fishing.

When I started fishing for steelhead in British Columbia a friend of mine, Michael Howard, introduced me to Bomber patterns tied by W.W. Doakes in New Brunswick. Their flies are so superior to any other Bombers that I have ever seen. After that introduction in the middle '80s I only fished with dry flies on the Clearwater and Snake rivers.

I realize that fishing either with the greased-line method where the flies are just under the surface or dry flies will often limit the number of fish that you catch but to me that didn't matter. I wanted to catch the fish under my terms and conditions only. For those that don't fish with dry flies I think they are missing a wonderful opportunity. To see one fish come up to a dry fly is better for me than hooking 10 that I can't see. I have taken fish on dry flies from water that I'm sure was at least 10 feet deep if not more. I fish the dry flies primarily waking where I cast about 45 degrees downstream, mend the line, and let it swim back. One of the most exciting aspects of this type of fishing is that about half of the time the fish misses the fly but will come back on subsequent casts. Waiting for that take is one of the most exciting things in fishing.

The first year that I stayed in Clarkston, Bob Weddell and I fished the Clearwater near Orofino and the Middle Fork of the Clearwater above Orofino very late in the season and the water temperatures were as low as 33, just above ice flowing in the river. We could only fish for 15 or 20 minutes at a time before we would have to get out of the water to warm ourselves. We were using greased-line fishing methods and would catch, on the average, one or two fish a day between us. Perk Lyda, a guide from Orofino, was fishing at the time in a jet boat with clients using shrimp for bait and we consistently caught as many fish as they did. He couldn't believe it.

One observation I had over the years was that there seemed to be a difference in how the fish would strike a fly. When I first started fishing we would get violent vicious strikes that we referred to as "depth bombs." They would hit so hard sometimes that on a few occasions I almost lost my balance and fell in. More often than not they would snap the leader and be off almost immediately. I quickly learned not to pinch the line when steelhead fishing because that would result in the hook being pulled out. You need to learn how to let the line go straight out from the reel without setting the hook.

Many times it was almost like you had a sixth sense in that you would notice something that was minutely different about the fly drifting in the water. At those times I would apply a gradual amount of pressure to set the hook. I think a lot of times those fish would put the fly in their mouth and just swim along before going down to the bottom.

Many fishermen don't realize that a lot of steelhead will hold next to the shore and in very shallow water. Many times fishermen wade out too far too soon and spook a lot of fish that are within easy casting distance.

Comet
(tied by Dave Clark)
Tail: Yellow and orange
Body: Gold tinsel
Hackle: Yellow and orange

The Comet without any bead head eyes was commonly used by Tom Morgan.

In later years I fished in British Columbia exclusively with a dry fly and I caught a lot of fish in 41-degree water. I have no doubt that you could catch fish in the Clearwater on the surface at that temperature. You can catch fish on the surface with a dry in a lot colder water than most fishermen will tell you.

I also found that if I could develop a good rhythm and cover a lot of water that I was a lot more successful. I tried to develop a rhythm where I would do one false cast, cast, move a little and cast again.

The other thing I found out over the years that helped me the most in catching steelhead on a fly was that I had to let go of my pre-conceived ideas. You need to put yourself in a frame of mind where you let the fish dictate your technique. You can't let yourself get in a frame of mind where you will only fish one type of water or one depth or one fly, etc.

My first Clearwater steelhead was caught just below the Potlatch Dam on the highway side. In the fall there was hardly any water running down that channel. About 50 yards below the dam was a small pool that held some steelhead. I was fishing late at night with a floating line and a Purple Peril when I caught a steelhead of about 8 pounds.

Actually, catching this fish was a bit of a letdown because it was so dark. However, I went back the next morning very early with my yellow Labrador dog. It was just starting to get daylight when I started fishing at the head of the pool. As I mentioned, there was not much water in that channel so the current in the pool was very, very slight. On one of the early casts a fish that seemed so big that I couldn't believe it broke the surface in a gentle head and tail rise taking my fly.

When it went dow, the tail seemed as wide as both of my hands spread out together. I set the hook and was fast to a monster. I'm sure that I fought the fish for 15 or 20 minutes before I heard someone shout from the road. I looked up and Keith was making his way towards me over the rocks in his suit. On his way to work he had seen me with a fish on and was coming to see for himself what it was. After some more time I was able to land it. Thirty-seven inches of the most beautiful fish that I had ever seen.

Other Memorable Fishing Stories

My most memorable fish of the many that I caught was on the Clearwater a couple of miles above Cherry Lane Bridge on the north side. I was fishing with my friend, Mac McPhetres, and I had started fishing the run just below where Pine Creek enters. Mac was fishing the rocks scattered in the river above the creek. I was using my 9 1/2' 6-weight graphite rod. For many this would be too light of a rod but, for me with my extensive experience catching large fish on light tackle, I didn't think so. I will explain in a minute why I don't think so.

I was fishing a Teeny nymph that Keith had given me. He had bought out a store's stock and had a large number of them. I had worked my way down only about a quarter of the run. At this point there is a current break caused by a rock structure under the water that is easily visible to the angler. I was fishing using the greased-line method with a floating long belly line mended to slow the fly as it worked its way around in the cast. As if in slow motion a large fish came up and took the fly as it skimmed along the surface. Even though it wasn't a dry fly it was working right on the surface.

I had learned long ago not to strike a fish when I saw them take the fly. If you do, particularly with a large steelhead, you will often break them off on the strike. I gently raised the rod and felt the heavy pull of a fish. Then I gave it a couple of good strikes to set the hook. Fishing with floating lines you can keep the hooks exceptionally sharp because they don't hit rocks on the bottom but I wanted to make sure that I didn't lose this fish.

When the fish felt the hook it made a screaming run to the other side of the river and headed downstream. I have always loved the sound of a click reel when a fish makes a run, so for many years I used a Hardy St. Aiden reel that is in their lightweight series with a click drag. To apply extra pressure all you have to do is brake the spool with your thumb on the inside.

I immediately started backing out of the water where I could follow this fish downstream. I knew that I wouldn't be able to hold it. The pool below where Pine Creek enters the Clearwater is long and very quiet after the additional headwaters area. There is hardly ever any brush or other similar obstacle in the river for a fish to get tangled in so I knew my chances of landing it were good. I carefully worked my way down the rock rubble that has been deposited below Pine Creek. Another great attribute of a click reel is that when you can't follow the fish because you are working your way downstream you can tell what the fish is doing by the sound of the reel.

I knew that I was into a large fish because I had seen it when it took the fly and now I could feel the heavy pulse of its tail as it hugged the bottom and fought the fly and line. After its initial run I kept a solid and heavy sideways pull on my rod with it parallel to the water. I had read of this technique in one of Joe Brook's books and had used it effectively against large fish many times. You usually see anglers hold the rod straight up while playing fish but this puts very little pressure on them. By holding the rod sideways they have to continually fight to stay in the stream and it wears them out much more quickly.

I continued to work down the run as I fought the fish. It jumped clear of the water several times. It was a magnificent fish. As I worked it in towards the shore I occasionally got a glimpse of it and could see that it was very big. While I was playing it a fellow angler across the river stopped his fishing to watch me. He called over to me and asked me what my name was. I told him. He continued to watch as I played the fish.

As I got the fish close to the bank I used a technique that I had developed while playing large fish on light tackle that enabled me to land them much faster than normal. I have always used lighter leaders than most anglers so I don't have a lot of margin and a big fish can easily break the tippet if you're not careful. From my experience with large fish, about 2/3 of the time is spent getting the fish close to the shore and the rest of the time getting it beached. As this fish got close to shore I moved my rod so that it was upstream of me and, again, horizontal to the river. I kept a steady pressure on the fish from this angle until it quieted down. Then I quickly reversed the direction of the pull by flipping the rod downstream while maintaining the steady pull. The fish gently swam into a little indentation in the bank and beached itself. I set the rod down and pounced on the fish. It was mine.

Here was the largest steelhead I had ever caught. At that time I didn't carry a tape but I set it alongside my rod and later measured the approximate distance. It was right at 40 inches! And a wild fish too. I quickly slipped the fish into the water and

gently held it for a few minutes while it regained its strength. I released it and it slowly glided away, becoming more ghost-like as it finally disappeared into the dark water. What a great feeling I had as I looked at the water where it had been. I felt so wonderful that I had caught the fish and returned it to the river to complete its spawning run and to help continue the great legacy of wild steelhead. Only the fish and I really knew that we had been together for a brief time. And it was free.

I didn't have a camera to record it and Mac was upstream so he didn't see it. The angler across the river had watched everything and saw me release it. He got in his car and continued up the river. A most interesting event took place that winter. Mac ran a sporting goods store in San Jose, California during the winter. As it happened, that winter a customer came in and was telling Mac about how he had seen Tom Morgan catch a big steelhead on the Clearwater River. Mac couldn't believe it. He said that he was fishing with me that day and he was just upstream. What a coincidence.

Another fish that was memorable was one of the last ones that I caught on the Clearwater. I was fishing with my good friend Earl Dorsey from Helena, Montana, on the run below Coyote's Fishnet. About two-thirds the way down the run on the far side is the swirl from a large rock below the surface of the water. I had been above the rock on the railroad tracks on a previous trip and had seen the run and knew it was probably eight to ten feet deep near the rock.

I was fishing a dark orange colored Bomber that was a similar color to the large fall caddis that hatches on the river late in the fall. Occasionally, as a caddis skims across a pool you will see a steelhead take one. The swirl above the rock, from the highway side where I was fishing, was a long cast and I could just reach it with my 9 1/2' 7-weight rod if I cast straight across the river.

On my first cast a small steelhead, probably in the 4-5-pound range, came up and made a pass at the dry fly. It missed it. I made another cast to the rock and there was the small steelhead again. Once more, it missed the fly. Since I was casting straight across in the beginning of the cast the fly was floating as a dead-drift dry fly. To some, having a steelhead come to a dry fly from a run 8 or 10 feet deep might seem unusual but I have had it happen a number of times. Not giving up easily I made a third cast and this time I clearly saw a big fish take the fly.

The fish disappeared with the fly and I tightened the line to set the hook. When I got it I, it was about 38" long. I don't know what happened to the small one but this one definitely wasn't what had made passes at the fly before.

Rod Building

I built my first fly rod when I was living in Clarkston, Washington. It was a fiberglass rod built on a Phillipson blank. It was the only fly rod that I ever built before buying Winston.

In my opinion, in order to be a great rod designer you must have a large range of fishing experience. It also helps to guide fishermen and to watch them fish and use a variety of rods. I think that presently most trout rods and steelhead/salmon rods are designed by tournament casters and are much too stiff. Many of today's rods are demonstrated at fishing shows and the ones that cast the farthest are the ones being made. Fortunately, most bamboo rod makers have not fallen into this trap and are still making rods that bend and flex appropriately for fishing situations. However, even some bamboo makers are leaning towards rods that are too stiff for good trout fishing. When I hear that a bamboo trout rod will cast all of the line I am very suspicious of its fishing action/stiffness.

Winston Rod Company

I was running the El Western Motel in Ennis, Montana in 1973. We had decided to sell the motel so I was looking for something to do. A good friend of mine, Al Wilson, was staying at the motel. He had been in the Army Air Corps with Doug Merrick, the owner of Winston, during World War II. Al said that Doug wanted to sell Winston. I had always had a passion for fly rods so thought this would be a great opportunity for me.

I immediately called Doug to see if he wanted to sell Winston. He said that he did and I told him that I was interested in buying it.

I made arrangements to fly to San Francisco to meet with him. On the way down I stopped in Salt Lake City to meet with my fishing friend, Sid Eliason, to see if he was interested in either loaning me money to help buy Winston or to become a partner. Sid said he would love being a partner with me.

I met with Doug and looked over the business. I must admit that I had stars in my eyes. Doug was like a God to me. I wanted Winston badly and told Doug that I would come back to Montana and make him an offer. He had five other people interested in the business so I offered him $10,000 more than he was asking to make sure I got Winston. Doug accepted my offer and Sid and I were the proud owners of Winston.

As mentioned before I grew up fishing a big variety of waters. This experience helped me develop a strong sense of rod types. Also using a variety of customer's rods let me see what others were doing and what worked best for different fishing conditions. When I first went to Winston there were only bamboo and fiberglass rods being produced.

The first thing I did was to design the Stalker fiberglass rods that were true #3 and #4 rods. There were very few light rods being made in the 1970s. Even in those days all of the fiberglass rods that I could find were much too stiff for the line designation they carried. The Stalker became an immediate hit and are still popular to this day. They never seem to come up on used-tackle sales.

Soon after I bought Winston, Fenwick brought out the graphite rods. They began to revolutionize not only the rod industry but also fly-fishing itself. It was not long before they completely took over the fly-rod business and forced fiberglass off the market. In my opinion, this did a great disservice to some of the fiberglass rods that were, and still are, great fishing rods. I also think that for many beginners graphite rods are easier to learn to cast with because their stiffness/speed fits their casting stroke.

By the time Fenwick brought out graphite rods, fiberglass had mostly replaced bamboo rods. Most of the bamboo-rod-making companies had closed their doors. The ease of making shafts from composite materials was much cheaper than making them from bamboo.

I am going to make a statement that will probably anger many bamboo rod makers. In my opinion, graphite is the best rod-making material to come along so far. Now, that is not to say that most graphite rods being made today are great rods. Far from it. There are more terrible rods being made today, in my opinion, than have ever been made at any other time.

However, graphite does offer the opportunity to make great rods. They are very lightweight, have great strength, won't take a set, have great design flexibility, have great casting range, and can be aesthetically pleasing if properly executed. I am very proud of the graphite rods that we are currently making and think that they are great fishing rods. They have supple tips, good flexibility, bend appropriately for trout fishing distances, and are beautiful.

This is not to say that bamboo rods are not also great fishing rods because many of them are. Bamboo is a great material and can be crafted into a beautiful rod that has an intrinsic value unequaled by any other material. Bamboo also has the benefit of being the traditional rod material that our fly-fishing sport was built upon. This gives it a tradition that won't ever be displaced.

However, just because a rod is bamboo doesn't make it a great fishing rod. I have always been very critical of any rod and whether they be bamboo, fiberglass, or graphite. Regardless of the material they must do the job well. In my opinion, bamboo is the most difficult material to design rods with. The weight of the material affects the rod action more than fiberglass or graphite. Therefore, it's critical that the tapers be worked out carefully and tested to insure that the rod performs well.

One of the great appeals for bamboo-rod makers is their ability to experiment with different tapers to develop a rod action that they prefer. With either graphite or fiberglass this design capability is not available to most amateur rod designers. Making bamboo rods can also represent an opportunity to develop not only tapers but also the other aesthetic design details of a rod.

When I was first looking at Winston to purchase it I intended to move the company to Montana. There were a lot of benefits to Winston in the Bay Area, such as the Golden Gate Angling and Casting Club, tradition of being in San Francisco, infrastructure of support businesses, and a big labor pool. Even with these benefits, I thought that a rod company should be in a great fishing area.

From Winston's beginning they produced a broad range of rod types from surf rods, boat rods, plug rods, to fly rods. When I bought the business most of the rods being sold were fly rods. Having been a spin fisherman for a number of years I could see that the spinning rods did not have great action. In addition, I didn't know anything about any other rods except fly rods. I also realized that most anglers wouldn't pay a premium price for spinning or boat rods even though the manufacturing costs were the same or higher than for a fly rod. Therefore, soon after buying Winston I dropped everything but fly rods.

Even though I liked San Francisco as a city I didn't want to live there. My heart was in Montana. Doug Merrick had agreed to work for me for 2 1/2 years to teach me the business. I decided that after he was through I would move Winston. By that time Glenn Brackett was working for me, and the two of us, at separate times, looked at different towns in Montana to move to. I had a very good knowledge of southwestern Montana that helped me look for an area.

The area around Twin Bridges, Sheridan, and Dillon appealed to me because of the good fishing and general lack of fishermen. The decision was made to buy the property and move Winston.

When the move was made to Montana, Winston was a very small company. Doug Merrick had already retired. We had the rod wrappers in the Bay Area and they stayed there while we sent rods back and forth. Glenn also did much of the wrapping. Al Wilson worked at his shop at home as he had been doing and we continued to send work back and forth. We had one part-time worker, Doug Wilson, who didn't move with us. Glenn Brackett, Chris Warner, and myself moved to Montana.

In the beginning Doug and I worked on the bamboo rods together. The next year Glenn came to work for me so both of us had an opportunity to work under Doug. However, during the time that we were in San Francisco we had another mentor, Gary Howells. I feel that Gary did more to help us develop our quality bamboo-making skills than anyone else did. He came over every Saturday morning and we talked extensively about bamboo rod-making.

When I bought Winston there were not established exact specifications for each rod. This was a big disappointment for me. In the beginning I did almost all of the taper pattern adjustments to develop our rod actions. I would work out the tapers, Al Talbot would cut the taper patterns, and then Glenn and I would glue up the sections, make the rods, and cast them. Al would then redo any taper pattern that I wanted changed. After considerable effort I had the most popular rod tapers well defined.

After the first year I took over running the milling machine to cut bamboo. I feel that I have a good mechanical aptitude and was very interested in machinery. Lew Stoner made the original milling machine. It is a very simple but elegant design that is the best that I have seen. It had oil bearings and a setting mechanism that was not as accurate as I wanted. Al Talbot made a new slide mechanism with a positive dial for setting the depth adjustment that worked extremely well. This machine was used for a number of years until we started to have trouble with the oil bearings. Then I rebuilt the milling machine adding a new ball-bearing spindle while retaining the adjusting mechanism that Talbot built.

After we moved to Montana and established our routine, each of us did specialized tasks, for the most part. In the beginning, I did most of the pole sorting and matching. Both Glenn and myself would do the sanding of the nodes. Glenn and I would do the cutting with me operating the milling machine and Glenn pushing strips into it. We would both check the strips for the quality of the cuts and final blemish inspection. Then when gluing, Glenn would spread the glue and I would run them through the binding machine. We would both work on straightening and hanging them.

Glenn did almost all of the section cleaning, rod ferruling, corking, wrapping, and wrap coating. He essentially took over the assembling of the finished bamboo rods. Glenn also did all of the repair work on bamboo rods. Glenn has assembled hundreds of bamboo rods and, in my opinion, is one of the great rod-makers today. He has a wealth of experience that just isn't available to most rod-makers today.

After the rods were ready for final finishing I would do that by spraying the varnish on in a special spray booth. The spray booth was set up with an exhaust fan, special dust-free filters, and I would wear dust-free clothing when spraying. I have always felt that spraying was the best way to apply the finish coat. By proper application, I could vary the varnish finish by the application rate putting on a lighter, thinner coat on the tips and a heavier one on the butts. Spraying is also very fast. I could varnish the final coats on ten two-tip rods in about three hours total, including setup and cleanup. The finish coats came out virtually perfect with almost no dust blemishes and these were easily polished out. I think that the finish varnish on our rods added greatly to the overall quality.

For most of the time that I owned Winston we casted every bamboo rod with both tips that went out of the shop. This not only gave us an opportunity to know what every rod that we sent out felt like, but it gave us a tremendous amount of casting experience with different bamboo rods. From my observations, the most difficult task for rod-makers is being able to cast a rod and determine its characteristics and how to change it for the better. This seems to only come with great experience.

Tom Morgan Rodsmiths

The goal of Tom Morgan Rodsmiths was to build the best fishing rod that was possible based on my experience and to encompass the appointments to make it the most beautiful that I could imagine. I also wanted the level of workmanship to be highest possible. I believe that this has been done. Anglers who have fished these rods constantly rave about their action and how beautiful they are. It has been very satisfying and rewarding to receive their accolades.

In the beginning I only was going to make a limited number of graphite rods in the lengths that I have always liked best along with reels that would complement the rods. The Hand Mill was not planned and only came about accidentally. However, the addition of the Hand Mill has been very rewarding and interesting for both Gerri and myself. One of the best parts of our business is the association that we have made with our customers.

I did not intend to make bamboo rods because I didn't want to make a milling machine to cut the strips. After the invention of the Hand Mill they could be easily made. Therefore, Gerri and I decided to add a limited number of rods to our graphite offering. I have always enjoyed making bamboo rods so it a natural addition.

My fishing experience and length of time in the fly-rod business allowed me to understand the product that I wanted to make. My associations with individuals in the fly-rod business provided me with the ability to get them to help develop the products that I wanted. I realize that for most people it would be much more difficult, if not impossible, to do this because of the limited production. As with most business startups, the initial time and costs were greater than I anticipated.

Gerri and I fell in love in 1993. We just celebrated our 8th anniversary and its been a fabulous time. When Gerri and I first started, my Multiple Sclerosis was getting quite severe but we always thought that it would stop before I got too disabled. I was able to cast the first prototype rods and develop the action that I wanted. Gerri and I both worked on the appointments on the rods, bags, and cases and she had many great ideas that we have incorporated.

Now that I am totally disabled, Gerri does everything except the rod blank and guide alignment. I still have a keen eye and between the two of us we get them "dead" straight. Fortunately for us, Gerri has the keen eye, the technical ability, and the desire to do what I consider to be the finest work in the industry. The workmanship on our rods is just incomparable.

Gerri will do much of the finish work on the bamboo along with the graphite. I do the design work and have assembled a group of casters that know what type of action I want to test the rods. Working on bamboo is a new experience for her, but she is looking forward to the challenge.

Bob Weddell

Bob Weddell of Orofino, Idaho caught hundreds of Clearwater steelhead on flies from the mid 1960s to the mid 1990s. This particular fish weighed 22 pounds and was caught in the 1970s.

During the course of our lives we occasionally cross paths with one of those truly "unforgettable characters." For me, Bob Weddell certainly falls into that category. After our first 20-minute conversation on the phone, I told him that I was going to scrap the idea for the book and just write an outdoor book starring him. After the first one thousand pages about fishing were completed, we would progress to the next 1000 pages about hunting. At some future date I would then write a book about the rest of the "local characters."

Bob is one of the last modern-day mountain men who really have an appreciation of the wild and pristine. He turns out to be one of my better sources of local fly-fishing history and helps me put a lot of the pieces together that I have gathered from other sources. Bob is almost 70 and has been an avid fly-fisherman for 50 of those years. He is 99.9% sure that he was the first one to use the greased-line technique on the Clearwater in 1967 and he has literally released thousands of steelhead.

Bob grew up in Northern California and obtained a fisheries degree from Humboldt State College in the 1950s. Bob was a long-time fishing partner of California's Bill Schaadt who even back then had attained legendary status as a salmon and steelhead fly-fisherman. Bob is friends with other notable fly-fishermen including Russ Chatham, Jim Adams, Woody Sexton, Stu Apt, Tom McGwaine, Glen Brackett, Tom Morgan, Keith Stonebraker, and the late Bill McAffee and Walt (Dub) Price.

Bob: I started steelheading in 1956 on the Eel and Russian rivers in California and the only reason I came to Idaho in the early 60s was to hunt and fish and to get away from the crowds in California. The thing that attracted me to hunting and fishing when I was a little crumb snatcher was the peace and solitude and the beauty. This was what it was all about. Then to see a lot of places turn into garbage where that doesn't even exist anymore drives me nuts.

The ultimate steelheading for me was in California and catching brandnew "chromers" that had just arrived from the salt. You're not talking about some spent fish several hundred miles inland that hasn't had a square meal for months. In my opinion, there has never been another steelhead fishery that could compare with a recently arrived Eel River fish fresh from the ocean.

Idaho was never a top-of-the-line fishery, ever, ever, it's just that every place else was deteriorating to the point where people started looking elsewhere. There's no coastal steelhead fly-fishermen that I'm aware of that would rate our waters high quality, except that here we have the summer fish which we didn't have on the coast. These summer fish are a sucker for that floating fly.

You have to ask yourself, why was Idaho basically the last state in the West to grow? It's because Idaho wasn't that good, most other states were better, but they all destroyed everything they had. No place could hold a candle to California in its day. It was a sportsmen's paradise. Idaho did have the big-game thing going for it elk, sheep, goats and deer. Idaho really didn't start to grow until about 30 years ago and then it exploded. The reason was that all the rest of the places were better, but as they destroyed themselves it just made Idaho far more attractive.

When I first came to Idaho in 1965 I almost got lynched one night at the Ranch Club in Garden City because I made the comment that I wanted to stop the Idahoan from the right to vote on matters that related to hunting and fishing.

When I first came to Idaho I worked for two years in the Health Department and I found out that the outfitters and guides in the Boise area liked to hang out at a watering hole called the Ranch Club in Garden City. I started going out there in the evenings and as I would sip my beer I would listen and write information down on the back of matchbook covers.

I eventually got well acquainted, and they all knew I was from California. My first year there I got my elk the first weekend, and then I got an antelope and a goat and a deer and a bunch of waterfowl. No one had ever heard of such a thing.

One of the regulars there by the name of Steve Jordan was an outfitter and one night he came up to me and asked me, "Bob, how would you like to do a float trip down the Salmon River?"

I said, "I'd love it, but I can't afford it." He told me it wouldn't cost me anything and I said "what's the hook?"

He said, "what do you mean?"

I said, "there's no free lunch in this world, what are you going to get out of it?"

He replied, "I would like to film you fly-fishing for steelhead."

I said, "Okay but I just have one question,"

He said, "What's that?" I said would you take this film out of the state of Idaho, and he said, "Oh yeah, Chicago, New York City, Los Angeles, everywhere," so I promptly told him where he could put his film.

Well we started yelling at each other and it started to escalate pretty fast. Pete, the owner, finally got us to settle down and this is what I told Steve, "Let me tell you something Steve, you people here in Idaho, you don't maliciously do things wrong but you don't have a clue about the outside world. There's a wall of humanity out there, I'm just the advance guard, what is going to happen in this state is something you will not believe. You people are sitting on an absolute fortune, you have a sportsmen's paradise for this day and age, and you don't have a clue of what you really have.

"Now you guys are talking about selling this out for ten cents because you don't understand the value of anything and if I had my way no native Idahoans would be allowed to vote on matters pertaining to Idaho." Man, you should have seen the whole bar rise up, one guy yelled, get a rope and I thought for a while that my life was in jeopardy.

The guides never get rich off these deals, they are a nickel-and-dime operation, they think they are cutting a fat hog and they can barely buy beans. Anyway, it really got wild for a while because here I was a mouthy Californian telling these guys this stuff.

Pete finally got things calmed down to where I thought I was going to survive the night and Steve asked me, "Bob, under your plan would we ever be allowed to vote if you were running things?"

I said, "Yep."

He said, "What would we have to do?"

I said, "All native Idahoans would have to leave for 3 years and go live in New York City, Chicago, or Los Angeles, then come back to Idaho and then you will realize what a glorious piece of real estate you folks really have."

That was about 1964-65 just before I came up here. They asked me when all this doom and gloom was going to happen, so I told them, it would happen within 10 years. Well, I moved up here to Orofino and didn't get back down to Boise for two years. I dropped in to the Ranch Club, and everyone wanted to buy me a beer and they all gathered around to catch up on what I had been doing.

Pete says, "You remember all that crap you laid on us a few years ago?"

I said, "Yea."

"Remember," Pete replied, "how you said it was all going to happen within 10 years."

I said, "Yeah."

Pete said, "Well, you were wrong."

And I said, "It hasn't been ten years yet."

Pete yelled, "No!, everything you said is already happening, and it's only been two years!"

As far as I'm concerned it's been tanking ever since. I can't believe the incredible mismanagement that I've seen. I haven't seen any common sense exercised. What you see on the river now is at best only a shadow of what it was.

Dub Price and Grease Lining

Walt Price was an artist from Seattle who started fishing the Grande Ronde with a group of guys from the Everett area in the mid 60s. I saw them fishing on the Grande Ronde in 67 and was amazed at how many fish they were catching. Even in those days there was a picket line of fishermen at the mouth of the Grande Ronde, most of them lure fishermen. The majority of them would wade out as far as they could and then throw those lures towards the middle of the river.

I watched Walt walk along the bank just dink casting between the shore and the fisherman that were out up to their chests. He never cast more than 15 feet and he was using a dry fly. I watched him catch several fish. It was the first time I had seen anyone use the grease-line method.

Bob Weddell caught hundreds of steelhead on a small Purple Peril.

Purple Peril
(tied by Bob Weddell)

Tail: Purple hackle fibers
Body: Purple wool with gold ribbing
Hackle: Purple
Wing: Wisp of partridge or similar feather

Well, we got talking in the evening and I mentioned to them that I had just come back from my first tarpon trip. I told them, "Do not allow yourself to go to the grave without doing the South Florida Keys tarpon trip. There's nothing on earth to match it."

So Walt piped up and asked me if I had a guide down there.

I said, "Yes, you have to have a good guide for the initial trip. A friend of mine is a tarpon guide by the name of Woody Sexton."

Dub says, "Woody Sexton! A good friend of mine is the closest of friends with Woody."

I said, "Who is your friend?"

Dub says, "Jim Adams."

I said, "Jim Adams! Jim and I went to school together."

I took a three-year break from school to go into the army so I could get the Korean GI bill. I was at Humboldt for two years and the army for three years. In my absence in the service, Walt Price came to Humboldt from Seattle. Walt was gone when I came back. Walt then asked me, "What's your name?"

And I said, "My name's Bob Weddell."

"Bob Weddell!" Walt exclaimed, "I've heard a lot of stories about you."

And I said, "Who you are you?"

And he says, "Walt Price."

And I said, "Walt Price! I've heard a few stories about you too."

At any rate, we just hit it off and Walt showed me how to catch those Grande Ronde fish using the greased-line technique. He was called Dub because he was an artist.

The next morning I drove into Clarkston to buy a floating line and I think that's when I called Stonebraker and told him I was getting this technique. "I'm in Clarkston," I told him, "and I'm on my way back to the Ronde."

I went back that day and Walt gave me some flies and I caught a lot of fish. Later that day Keith showed up and watched us fishing. I always give Keith a hard time and tell him he looked like a coyote in the sagebrush observing this new technique.

I had already fished the Clearwater for one season before I met Walt, but I was using the west coast technique. I was catching fish but had nothing to compare with what Dub had showed me. The next day after leaving the Ronde I went home and tied up a few flies.

Walt asked me if I was going to try the new method on the Clearwater and I said, "What do you think?" The first time I tried grease lining on the Clearwater was the day after I left the Grande Ronde. I went to one of my favorite spots and I could see a rig parked on the highway side, so I went and turned around and parked and here the Walt Disney guys were just coming up out of there.

Ed Ward was one of them and Milt Kahl and Ken Anderson. As they were coming out I was going in for the first attempt at grease lining on the Clearwater. I asked them, "Did you guys do anything?" and they said, "no but we did have one grab," and I said "it's nice to know that there is a fish there." So I went down and it was either the first or second cast on a bright sun-lit day at noon, and my reel just started screaming. I remember thinking, Oh my God, this is unreal.

I wrote Walt Price a letter in Seattle and told him about it and we corresponded for a while but I never saw Walt in person again. The term grease lining is obsolete any more because we don't grease the line anymore. These guys with their sink-tip lines aren't grease lining. If a guy is grease lining and puts a split shot in front of the fly, he's no longer grease lining, in fact I take them all the way to bait fishing when you have a split shot on the line.

I go along with lead in the tying of the fly if you want to get down or use a bigger hook. After I caught my first fish grease lining on the Clearwater I wasn't about to go rushing back to the Ronde when I had the Clearwater all to myself.

Weddell Introducing Duke Parkening to grease lining
Anyway, I knew Duke Parkening was in the area. He was building his home on the Middle Fork. I had met Duke for the first time on the lower Eel in the fall of 1959 after I returned from the army to go to college.

Well, once I started doing this thing with the grease line I intentionally let it slip to Perk Lyda who was guiding on the North Fork. I told Perk, the next time you see Duke let him know I have a whole new technique for catching steelhead, it's so deadly I won't even discuss it in public. I knew Perk would pass the information to Duke and it wasn't even 24 hours later that Duke was knocking on my door at a cabin I was living in up Orofino Creek. I had already made up my mind that I was going to give it to him because it was going to get out sooner or later.

We chatted for a while and he says, "Could I just go with you tomorrow and watch?"

I said, "Sure Duke."

He asked, "Are you going to fish tomorrow?"

I said, "Yes."

He said "Where should I meet you?"

And I said, "Let's meet at the slaughter house run at 11:00 or 12:00."

He said, "How about 6:00?"

And I just said, "Are you kidding, I'm not getting up that early. "

You have to realize in those days you didn't have to beat anyone because no one else was fishing. I usually didn't start fishing till about 1:30. I wasn't having any of this break-the-ice business. Finally I agreed to meet him at 9:00. In the morning I get to the hole and Duke is already there pacing back and forth.

I still had the rod together from the day before and I said, "Duke, it's unbelievable how easy this technique is." I went up to the head end and I said, This is all it is, Duke," and I popped a little 70-foot cast. "You will see it coming around like this," I said "and if there happens to be a fish in here he's going to grab it right about now." And when I said that, a huge fish grabbed that fly and took off down the river. Duke went out of his mind. As soon as I said "Now," the reel was screaming.

Then we made another stop up river. Duke was still following me around. I walked into the top end and within two casts was into a fish. I get the fish in, release it, make another cast and boom, another fish and then another fish. Duke finally couldn't take it any longer and he raced back to his rig and pretty soon he comes running back across the gravel.

By the time he got back up to me, I told him that it was all over.

He says, "What are you talking about?"

I said, "They're gone."

He said," How do you know?"

I said, "because I just made another cast through there and I didn't catch a fish." It was hilarious, but that is the story about how Duke got started with the greased-line technique.

I also introduced Glen Brackett right away into grease lining. Glen was working for the Fish and Wildlife Service up in Spokane. That was before the Winston Rod days. Him and his wife Gloria would come down on weekends and move into my cabin. Glen was an old ex-Humboldter and he fished for salmon on the Smith River. I believe Glen is the one who got me started on riffle hitching. I got into the habit of riffle hitching and the majority of fish I have caught for the past several years on my little purple fly have been riffle hitched.

The Clearwater steelhead is not a rocket scientist type of fish. When you have an aggressive one of these fish you have to work awfully hard to keep them off the fly rod. I have caught fish on flies that were just hammered.

Back in the 1960s I used to grease my floating line at least a couple of times a day. I'd make a cast ever so slightly downstream and a simple upstream mend. Just a simple lift over. The rod is horizontal and you are pointing the rod at the fly. Sometimes I have found if the water temperature is fairly warm and if you have a lethargic fish, I will put a downstream mend to slow the speed of the fly down. Basically it is just staying with the fly and when the grab comes, never hang on to the line. Most of these fish just take off, they are very explosive and they hook themselves. Sometimes at the end of the swing I might work the fly with 2-3 pulls just in case one was following it. But I like to get the fly back in, take two steps and cast again. I never make two casts to the same position unless I have raised a fish.

Steelhead don't often move great distances to hit a fly but once in a great while you will have one of these that looks like a shark come grab a fly. One time I had a fish come to the fly 12 out of 13 casts. I never got the hook into him and caught him on the 14th cast with the same fly. Every time I could see his dorsal fin cutting through the water. When that happens on the Clearwater it's a good idea to rest the fish for 10-20 seconds. You have to figure out the rhythm similar to what you see when a brown trout is feeding on mayflies. A brown comes up in a regular sequence and if you cast too early nothing will happen. On the Snake that's not the case because they tend to move more, so there I move up a little and try to anticipate where they are moving.

On the Snake if you get a pull the chances of that fish holding is much less because those fish on the Snake are usually moving. They move at the pace of a slow walk, so if you have a grab and it's a miss you've got two things to do. What I normally will do depending on the piece of water and how bad I want to fish. I'll wait just a moment and take 2-3 steps and cast and if nothing happens get out of the river and run like hell. Get up above them and start chopping down through and hope you contact them. But where you can really see them moving and they are very subtle, you have to be watching for them.

I want to tell you something I have known about the Snake River for several years and it was verified again to me this last fall (2003) by my friend Bill Henry from Afton, Wyoming. The Snake is a big river and when you fish it for the first time the immediate reaction is that you need a large fly. Let me tell you something. if you know the water and are a decent fisherman you will get 2-3 times more action using smaller flies. Those fish will inhale the small fly and just bang a large fly around.

I just received a note from Bill Henry who has fished the Snake for several years. He said one day this last fall he hooked five wild steelhead in one and one half hours. The fish had refused a number eight Green Ant so he put on a number 10 Blue Charm and proceeded to hook all those fish.

I remember something Bill Schaadt used to say, Bill didn't care what kind of feather was at his table. Of course I'm talking winter fish. Bill would say, the guy who's going to catch the most fish is the guy who has his fly in front of the most fish the longest amount of time. Period! Bill would fish a little black fly with a little gray tail or an orange fly with a black tail; he didn't care about the fly.

I loved his fly box, we both smoked Camels, Bill at the end of the day his eyeballs would be down to his cheeks tying up a batch for the next day and he would take a pack of Camels and take the cellophane wrapper off and put the flies in it, roll it up and put it in his shirt pocket. I developed the same habit myself. I always have to laugh when I get next to one of these blue bloods who are displaying one of their works of art and I always enjoyed going to my pocket and pulling out my Camel packet of flies and saying, I think I will try this one.

I developed what I call my little purple fly; it is similar to a low water Blue Charm that Walt Price showed me. My pattern is a purple wool body with a small silver rib, a red tail, a black hackle and a mallard flank feather for the wing. I am a firm believer in white for the wing. I am also a firm believer in size of pattern. I base the size of pattern on the particular run and if you want to catch a lot of fish you need to use the smallest pattern you can. You will have action on a bigger fly but they seem to grab the smaller flies better. That is the only fly I have used for several years, just that one pattern, patterns are not that important.

On the Snake I used to fish a #6 wet fly with a small dropper. The small fly produces a lot better than the larger fly, they like to play with the larger flies. You have to remember that you are dealing with a creature that uses it eyes for a living; they don't have any problem seeing the smaller flies.

A steelhead takes a fly exactly opposite of a salmon; the hook is turned away from the fish. One time I missed a big fish on the Skykomish River in Washington and I studied and pondered what had happened to make me lose that fish. I was sick about missing it because I was told I couldn't grease line one of those Skykomish fish. I'm looking at the fly and dragging it across and I said crap, I've got that hook canted away from the fish.

I decided to tie a couple of half hitches right on the shank right below the hook. With this kind of riffle hitch you don't have to worry about which side of the river you are on. You put that hitch right by the eye, all it is, is a double half hitch and you cinch it up right underneath in the throat. Don't cinch it up on the side because it will cant the hook away from the fish. If you cinch it up underneath, the hook is straight with the current.

Glenn who loved to riffle hitch did it a little bit different. He tied his flies on heavy wire hooks in sizes 2's and 4's. He ties his riffle hitches at the side. To vary the action he will tie the riffle hitch farther toward the bend of the hook which creates a significant wake. Since then I riffle hitch about 99% of the time. You will catch more fish with a smaller slimmer fly that you will with a Bomber. I would rather take one fish on top than 30 underneath.

When I first started steelheading I thought the secret was going to be in the pattern so I experimented a lot. If I was fishing winter fish I would use a larger-sized Popsicle pattern with the marabou. I would use a 2/0 hook with a floating line.

I like to catch fish a long ways out. A lot of my casts are hernia casts, tip toes and hernias. I have no interest in catching steelhead close to shore. When you first step into the water you just free your hook from the keeper and let it go clunk, then it's two pulls and another clunk and just keep doing that until you can't cast any farther. Once you are throwing, as far as you can, then take two steps down and cast out again as far as you can. You have already swept the close water clean. One to two steps after each cast and move through quickly.

Clearwater Steelhead

Winter steelhead are more of a hunt-and-peck thing because they move into that deeper slower water. It's harder to find the real meat buckets in the winter. But for the grease-line technique and summer fish all a person has to do is think trout more than anything without the upstream presentation. And use an attractor-type fly. With steelhead it's more of a predatory strike.

People in this country are scared to death of dirty water. For instance the Russian River on its clearest day of the year would never have visibility much over what the Clearwater is on a dirty day. But then you ask how far a steelhead is going to move in the first place, not very far. These local people, good heavens, if the river gets the tiniest bit off then they are gone, they don't fish. Well, if you knew what you were doing you would be fishing that much harder because the more off color the water is, the better it is because if you get the fly in a fish's window before he even sees it he's going to grab it a heck of a lot faster than if he can see it coming 20 feet away.

All I ever used was 8-pound-test leaders. A lot of guys don't realize it, but the leader when it comes to casting is very important as far as turning over and so on. One day Jimmy Green asked me what I thought about the butt of the leader and I said I think that's the most important part of the leader and he said, 'So do I, how long do you think it should be?' and I said, 'Long, 4-5 feet, and he said, 'yes.' I use a long butt, and then short, short, short and then a long tippet for a 10 ft leader. I just feel more comfortable with a 10-foot leader. It allows you to keep the fly further away from the line. I don't put floatant on my line because the riffle hitch pops it right on top. When you tie the riffle hitch, use two half hitches and keep in mind when you put the head on the fly you want a narrow place behind the fly for the riffle hitch. You just do a half hitch, lay it up, cinch it up underneath, lay another half hitch putting it over the first one. The second half hitch is always behind the first.

Big Steelhead

As far as the biggest, all I can do is estimate, I know where it was, it was a great big female. It was an awfully, awfully big fish. I did not measure the fish because with a big one I get more concerned because it takes longer to release them. I remember exactly where I released it, fortunately I had a place where it was long run but there was a back eddy where I landed it. I remember looking at it. I had worked two summers with Fish and Game in Crescent City and have handled thousands of commercial-caught salmon, I'm very good at estimating size and I figured it was close to 28 pounds.

One year I kept a fish on the Snake that was 39 1/2 inches and it weighed 19 1/2 pounds, but it had that snaky look it because it was one of those winter-time fish. But this fish I caught on the Clearwater that I thought was 28 pounds was an October fish and had that deep girth to it. This was what was intriguing me because I've been into lots of 18- to 22-pound fish. Every year I would catch a few that were over 40 inches.

I was fishing in the Lenore area one afternoon on a piece of water I had put together. I had just started fishing when I heard another rig stop on the other side of the highway. My hackles immediately went up and I wondered who in the hell was interfering with my fishing.

It was Pettit and Stonebraker and when they saw me they yelled, "You SOB, we drove all the way from Lewiston and you're fishing in our water."

I got a lot of satisfaction when I yelled back and said, "Now you bastards have a wee idea of what I have been trying to tell you, now don't bother me because on the next cast I am going to hook a fish."

Stonebraker thought that was the funniest thing he had ever heard and Pettit asked me if I was serious. When I said that I was 100% serious Pettit ran back to his rig to get his camera. Stonebraker was going crazy and couldn't believe that Pettit was taking me serious.

When he got back with his camera, I told him to focus on a spot 95-100 feet below and I would tell him exactly when to depress the shutter. Stonebraker still couldn't believe that Pettit was falling for this line of BS.

I cast straight out and as I held the rod in one hand I was giving Pettit directions with the other. Not yet, not yet, and as the fly came across I yelled at Pettit to take the picture just as a large steelhead inhaled the fly. Pettit has the original photo, I have a copy that is faded, but if you look close you can see the snout of the fish come up out of the water.

It was a big fish and I ended up running down river a third of a mile. Pettit and Stonebraker didn't hang around, they took off fishing. What I didn't tell them was that fish had risen to the fly 3 or 4 times on previous casts. Every time the fish was late and behind the fly. This told me that there was an aggressive fish in that piece of water and all I had to do was to throw a little mend in the line to slow the fly down so the fish wouldn't miss it.

Jim and Carol Green

Carol and Jimmy Green at their home above the Grande Ronde in 2002.

Jim had been telling me much of his life story and steelhead fly-fishing experiences all afternoon in his home high above the Grande Ronde. He ends our conversation with this comment: "I believe that the really true fly-fishing is fishing a dry fly for trout. You have to have skill to cast and allow the fly to float with no drag and you need to use a fly that at least approximates the size of a natural insect. You have to be aware of the river and exercise skill in setting the hook when the fly disappears."

Jim was one of the fly-fishing fraternity's true legends, and a regional, if not national, treasure. His contributions, ranging from rods constructed from fiberglass, graphite and boron to floating lines, and ferrule modifications, have revolutionized the sport and we haven't even mentioned his two-handed graphite rods which he introduced a short time ago.

He was a former world champion and national champion fly-caster, and many of the protocols and rules that govern that sport were a direct result of his efforts and dedication.

His wife Carol has also won several casting competitions and for many years has been considered one of the nation's better fly casters. Jim passed away in 2004.

Jimmy: I've never been a nut about patterns. I love to fish because I love to cast. Getting caught up in all that nonsense about what fly to use was never my thing. When it comes to fishing, casting is a lot more important to me than fly selection. Don't get me wrong, I appreciate the work and effort of fly tiers and many of the traditional flies are real works of art, it's just something that I never really got into.

However, having said that, I do have a preferred set of flies. I like to fish the Green Butt Skunk, the Purple Butt Skunk and variations of that fly. The main variation that I came up with years ago is to eliminate the white wing and replace it with black. I like purple flies, but mostly I just use whatever flies I happen to have in my box. Most of my flies have been tied by others and many of my friends keep me well supplied.

When I ask Carol about favorite patterns she laughs and says, "Anything I can con off any other fisherman. We used to tie our own flies but I don't have time anymore and when we have such nice amiable friends that have flies I am more than happy to use them. I really don't have a favorite pattern, but I happen to like flies that have Flashabou in them and I happen to like small dark flies that are variants of the skunk."

We start talking about surface flies and they say they haven't done much of that. They smile at each other as Carol starts a story. "We were fishing for steelhead and Jimmy put me in front of him, he let me go down the river first with a dry fly and I'll be darned if I didn't get a roll from a fish. It was a really nice roll so I worked it and worked it and I got him up another two times, but couldn't get the fish to hit that fly to save my life, but it sure liked to roll on it.

I finally gave up and moved down and I'll be darned if I didn't get another good swish from a fish, but again I can't even touch it. Jimmy is coming up behind me. "They both start laughing, "Jimmy is supposed to have a dry fly too, and he's hooking all these fish and he finally got my goat when at the end of the day I found out he was using a Skunk and using me for a fish finder. I don't think I have used a dry fly since.

Bob and Beverly Black

Jimmy: Our good friends Bob and Beverly Black from Oregon have fished the Grande Ronde for 35 years. Beverly Black has caught hundreds of steelhead on the Grande Ronde, more than any other woman I know.

I consider Bob to be one of the most accomplished fly-fishermen I know. Bob loved to catch steelhead on a dry fly and he would fish a lot of Bomber patterns with a riffle hitch to create a wake. We fished the lower river in the evenings and I always let him go first with the dry and I would follow with a wet. There were a lot of times when the fish would roll on his fly two or three times and then it would stop. Bob would move down a little farther and now of course that fish was my fish and Bob knew it. He just didn't want to catch a fish with a wet fly.

I would use a small dark fly like a Skunk, a pattern without the white wing on it, I used all black-bear hair and of course on the first cast I would hook that fish that was raring to grab something a couple of inches under the water. That's the way Bob Black and I fished together, we had a lot of fun. That's how we used to team fish.

I always thought that if I was a millionaire I would hire a guy to go out there in the water with no hook on the fly and raise the fish for me and then I would go out and catch the fish.

Ted Trueblood

One of my best friends was the well-known outdoorsman and writer Ted Trueblood. I met Ted in California and fly-fished for shad with him on the Russian River. After that trip we started going to Henry's Lake and the Henry's Fork for a week each year. One year we fished the Henry's Fork for a whole week and

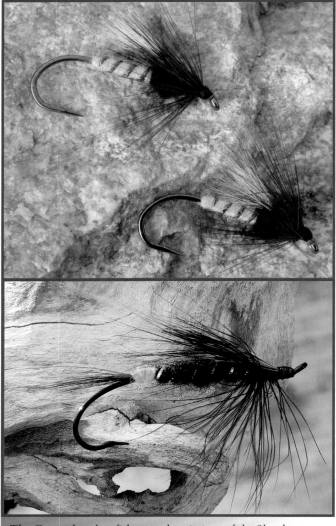

The Greens loved to fish several variations of the Skunk.

Skunk Patterns
(Top flies tied by Jerry Cebula)
(Lower fly tied by Terry Nab)

Tail: Red hackle fibers
Butt: Green
Body: Black with ribbed silver tinsel
Hackle: Black
Wing: White bucktail

had the river to ourselves. It was unbelievable, but that was several years ago.

Ted introduced Carol and I to the Grande Ronde in the mid 1960s. We would come over to the Lewiston valley for a few weeks and fish the Snake, Clearwater, and Grande Ronde. Ted and I were probably the last two fly-fishermen that fished for steelhead on that section of river that was inundated by Lower Granite Dam in 1972. That was some of the best steelheading water in the United States. All of those fish that were headed for the Clearwater, Grande Ronde, Imnaha, Salmon and other rivers had to pass through there. You could fish from the shore and some of my best memories are from that area. I believe that was the last time I ever fished with Ted before he passed away.

Rod building

Carol: I was introduced to fly-fishing when we got married. I mean it was either that or sit at home. That was 40 years ago. It was strictly a case of join in or sit it out and I am an active person and I can't stand to watch people do things. Jimmy taught me basically to fly-cast on our honeymoon when I was still a "yes, dear" person." I grew up in the south fishing with a cane pole but I thought that was boring. Jimmy taught me how to cast and I went right into tournament casting right then and there. I like 10 1/2 foot rods. I have a 5-weight and a 9-weight. Jimmy made them specially for me out of boron.

Jimmy interjects, "Boron was hard to work with, it was heavier than graphite. It seems like today the main criteria for a fishing rod is to make them as light as possible.

Carol: "I like a balanced rod, I want one where the reel and rod complement each other. I really don't like these light, light things. I like a rod that bends all the way down but I also want the power in the tip. It takes an expert like my husband to even make me one. I want a precise rod which means tippier, it needs to have a little slower action. Jimmy might contest that.

Jimmy: "With a rod, the most important part is to make the tip correct. The tip is the most important part in determining action as far as I'm concerned. It has to bend in a certain manner and once you have that in the tip of the rod then you can put different kinds of butts on these tips to make the rod stiffer or slower. Carol likes a fast-tip rod because she likes the rod to bend down in the butt.

Carol: "When we traveled around tournament casting we would fish. That's when we came up into this part of the country and there were no casting clubs around and so we went fishing instead of tournament casting and since I have been fishing I prefer the long rods."

Carol: I dearly love to fly-cast and I dearly love to fish, I just can't quite find a place to fish anymore. It's just getting harder for me to fish, I've been thinking about it and I'm basically giving up steelhead fishing. There's too many people, you can't find a place to get in.

One day I was down on the Snake trying to find a place to get on the river. I went all the way to Asotin and every place I knew where there might be fish was taken not only by one or two but three or four different people and I finally went back to this one place but I didn't think there would be a fish there, mainly because there were 3 boats across the river and they were all catching fish. I thought that meant that all the fish must be on the other side of the river and not on this side.

So I decided to practice my casting. Well I'll be darned if on the second cast I caught a fish. Nobody that I knew of had ever caught steelhead in this place, even the boats were on the other side of the river. I landed the fish, let it go and I made two more casts and I had another fish on. I caught four fish in less than an hour.

That place has never been empty since. I haven't been able to get back on it. The boats are right there next to shore now. The trouble on the Snake is the boats will see a fly-fisherman catch a fish and pretty soon they are going back and forth not ten feet away from the bank.

Just this last year I was out there and there were three boats out near the middle of the river. I made a long cast and I hooked a rock. The rock felt darn good. It was the first hit I'd had all year. Anyway, I came back on it just to see if it was going to shake

its head or not, it didn't, and so I jerked and it came off, the fly swung around and I made a couple of more casts. By the time I made two more casts, there was a boat down below me, a boat directly across from me, and a boat right above me. They saw me hook up on that rock and thought I had a fish and the sad part is, I could have put a fly in every one of those boats, they were that close. Those boats could go anywhere, that's the sad part, so as a result I think from now on I will confine my fishing to bass fishing. That's fun fishing.

Ronde Story

Jimmy: I fished the lower Grande Ronde one fall evening about 2/3 of the way down the confluence. There were two other anglers in the run with me. As we were moving through the hole all three of us hooked fish at the same time. The water was very clear and when I looked down I could see a large school of steelhead swimming up river. They were all around us, those fish were swimming between our legs.

In the next hour and a half I landed 18 steelhead and the other two fishermen did the same. We quit when it got dark but I knew that those fish would be holding in the lower Grande Ronde and that the next day should be great fishing. I got up early in the morning and fished the lower river and didn't get a fish. I then realized that those fish were probably Salmon River fish and they were long gone.

I dispute the notion that steelhead will not readily move to a fly when on the move. One day on the Snake River I could see some fish rolling a long ways down river. I hadn't had any luck so I stopped to watch them. They continued to jump and roll as they got closer and closer. As soon as they came within casting range I hooked a fish on the first cast and then landed two more. Then they were gone. Those fish were moving upriver very quickly and they readily came to the fly.

Two-handed Rod Evolution

When we were living in Long Beach, California I met John Olin who owned Winchester Arms. He was a multi-millionaire who owned horses that had won the Kentucky Derby three times. He was a member of the famous Moisie Atlantic Salmon Club. John called me at Fenwick and told me that he was getting tired of casting his 10 1/2 foot bamboo rod and asked me to build him a lighter weight rod. John sent the bamboo rod to me and I used that as a template to build John a fiberglass rod.

John loved the rod and invited me to be his guest at the Moisie Club. He sent me the tickets to fly to St Louis, put me up in a fancy hotel and the next day a private jet with myself as the only passenger flew to Canada. When we landed at the airport, a helicopter was waiting to fly me to the river. Fishing was done out of 20 foot canoes and two gaffers waited on each fisherman. While I was there I gave casting lessons to many of the members. I fished as a guest at the club for seven straight years until John passed away.

You could only belong to the salmon club if you were a multi-millionaire. They would hire over 85 people to wait on them, guides, gaffers, cooks. There were 15 members in the club and they had 85 people to wait on them. Many times the gillies would cast and hook the fish and then hand the rod to a member. Many of the members were old and feeble so the gillies would do a lot of the work.

Women were not allowed to be members of the club; it's a men only club! Women were allowed to visit but even wives were not allowed to eat in the dining room with their husbands. It's still that way today.

Carol: One poor old guy died and left his wife his membership in the club and one of the members was heard to say, "We'll get rid of that old broad soon" and this lady was paying umpteen thousands of dollars a year to belong and every time she went there it cost her $1000 dollars a day just for the privilege of having people wait on her and she wasn't even allowed to eat in the dining room!" I can tell this is a sore subject with Carol.

Jimmy says that she did have a nice place to stay and that usually several of the men were very nice and would eat with her and keep her dinner company.

"How sweet of them," Carol says.

"I went myself," Jimmy says, "Even John Olin ate with her and he didn't even like women!"

Jimmy: Every night two of you were assigned where you would fish in the morning and afternoon. Once you were assigned to a pool that water was yours, no one else could fish there during your time, even if you chose not to fish. The rules only allowed you to start fishing at 9:00 in the morning and at 1:00 in the afternoon. Some of the guys wouldn't start fishing till ten or eleven but of course I would be down there at nine.

You weren't allowed to carry any of your stuff down to the canoes, the gaffers did that. The only thing I wouldn't allow them to do was to tie on my own fly, I figured I could do that. John Olin would give everyone a kit of flies and that's what we would use.

Do you know what the greatest sound in the world is? It's the sound of those two men in the canoe working in unison as the paddles cut through the water and make that swishing sound. Swish, swish, me sitting in that canoe listening to that sound as they took me to my fishing spot was something I will never forget. That had to be the greatest sound on earth.

One year, the Duke of Wellington came from England to fish with us. He was quite the Englishman. I'll never forget the Duke's wading staff, it was made out of some hard-polished wood and the handle was carved out of ivory and was intricately carved. When he fished he had a tweed suit, tie and matching hat.

One day the two of us were assigned to the same pool. He used a heavy 15-foot, two-handed bamboo rod. I had seen these in casting tournaments, but I had never seen anyone fish with one. As we would take turns casting, the Duke kept telling me why the European two-handed rods were a lot better than the single rods that Americans used. He made fun of the Americans who were constantly having to double haul and false cast to get the distance they needed.

He told me that his two-handed rod was better because there was no back-cast or false casting involved and he didn't have to double haul. He let me try it out and I caught some fish with it. Right away I could see how easy it was to mend the line and I liked the extra distance.

That experience with the Duke got me to thinking. I was designing rods for Fenwick at the time and after that trip I went home and started building the first fiberglass two-handed rods that I am aware of. The Europeans may have had them, but I knew of no one in the United States that was using them. I built them for the members of the Moisie Club and didn't market

Frog on the banks of the North Fork River.

them for the general public. Some of those rods are still being fished at the club today.

Jim pauses and Carol continues, "Actually all of this two-handed business came about from me. I hate it, but it came from me. I tried to teach my friend Joanne Strobel how to cast for three years off and on. She had had a broken wrist and she wanted to steelhead fish. Well, you know if you get a 9-foot steelhead rod with a number 8 or 9 line that is capable of fishing the Thompson or any of the big rivers it requires a lot of strength and she just couldn't do it. After a while I got tired of trying to teach her. She knew what she was supposed to do but just did not have the strength to do it. She was only 5' 1".

Anyway, I got exasperated one day and said, "Jimmy would you make her a two-handed rod?" At that time two-handed rods were just used in Europe, there was nothing here in the U.S. Jimmy had built a few fiberglass two-handed rods for the club, but no one else had seen them.

Well, Jimmy made this two-handed graphite rod just before we were going over to the Skagit to fish. I took the rod to Joanne and we went over to the park and she started trying out this rod and lord, she was casting immediately. She was easily casting 80-90 feet. Well, I'll be darned if Harry Lemire and some others didn't come along and they are watching Joanne and they can't believe what they are seeing.

Pretty soon there was a whole line of people there watching and after about 10 minutes Harry asked to try it. Before you knew it everyone was trying it out and Joanne never saw it for the rest of the day. All these men are out there trying it and that's basically how the big deal in two-handed rods started over there on the west side. That was the first graphite two-handed rod, the one he built for Joanne."

"I made those first graphite two-handed rods," Jim says, "at the same time I built Carol's graphite/boron rod in the 1970s. I had a group of fishing friends that would come over to my house and we would spend hours at my casting pond experimenting with my designs. We experimented with different lengths, weights, lines and lots of other things. I was still fishing a single-handed rod at that time, but I started taking a two-handed rod with me and used it a little on the Skagit and Thompson rivers. Our group started using them and pretty soon a friend of a friend wanted one and so we started marketing them.

I didn't like the way those first rods cast. I couldn't seem to get a long cast without having to work really hard. One time, when I was doing all this experimenting I was preparing to go on a fly-fishing trip to Florida with Lefty Kreh. Lefty and I are good friends and we would fish for tarpon with #12 long-bellied lines that were very heavy.

On a whim one day, just before I was going to go to Florida, I put that heavy saltwater line on a two-handed rod and could not believe how well it could cast. The problem all along had been that I wasn't using heavy-enough lines. Since that time I have determined that 40-45-foot shooting heads are ideal and with a little flip you can easily cast a fly 70 feet. I don't normally cast over 100 feet with my two-handed rod but I have cast a line 150 feet in my back yard."

Carol: It takes a good caster to single-hand cast, they don't have to be good with a two-handed rod. That's one of the reasons we have a lot more people on the water.

Jimmy interjects, most of the people we see on the Ronde can't do a double haul which is very strange, and nobody seems to want to improve their casting. You can't believe the people we watch here that don't know how to cast. I would say about 80% don't know how to cast. I can't understand it, they say they like to fly-fish yet they won't improve on their casting."

Carol: It's because they catch fish on a small stream and don't feel they need to get better. I basically think a two-handed rod is for 60 and senile," she laughs, "but that's just my opinion. I'm a single-handed person when I'm fishing. Jimmy has these casting games that he forces me into and I use the two-handed rod then and only then. I don't like them. They have taken all the beauty out of fly-casting. A single-handed rod with a good caster is poetry in motion. With a two-handed rod anybody can swish it out there and get out there 80-90 feet with no knowledge at all, just a big swish.

The problem with a lot of women trying to fly-cast for steelhead," Jimmy says, "is that they don't have enough strength and they get tired with a single-handed rod. They don't like to wade out too far like the men do so it can become kind of scary for them fishing for steelhead.

The alternative is to get a two-handed 13 foot or 14 foot rod and make a shooting head just like one you would use for a single-handed rod. Just because you buy a two-handed rod doesn't mean you have to be a Spey caster to fish, that's a lot of baloney. Anyway, you can take the same darned line that they were using on a single-handed rod and put it on a two-handed rod as long as the rod is not too powerful, Carol could have them casting in 15-20 minutes and have them casting 60-80 feet where they can catch fish all day long and do it easily without wading out too far.

I love two-handed rods because I get a kick out of them, but I don't Spey cast. When I'm fishing I use what I call the aerial Spey. When the line swings downstream I pick it up over my left shoulder and I pivot and cast across. I call it the aerial Spey because it doesn't go over the bank and I don't have to worry about hitting rocks or brush or anything. You learn to pick it up quick and you are out their already. If you go through all that Spey casting and move your line this way then that away and swing it around and swish the water you scare every fish in the world. I think it's ridiculous. But the guys like it and they think if you buy a two-handed rod you gotta Spey cast. I just think they're crazy. I can follow any two-handed man that's Spey casting and cast 30 feet farther.

Keith Stonebraker

Keith Stonebraker is one of the area's premier steelhead fly-fishermen and resides in a home overlooking the Clearwater River.

Keith Stonebraker is one of the original local steelhead fly-fishing pioneers and is considered to be one of the better local steelhead fishermen. He also served an eleven-year stint on the Idaho Game and Fish Commission. Keith was born in the shadow of the Blue Mountains in Dayton, Washington, but has spent his whole life in the Lewiston Valley. He earned a college degree in zoology, "Something I couldn't get a job in," he says. He admits that he has never fished for steelhead in the Touchet or Toucannon rivers which are near Dayton but would like to do it someday.

I doubt that will happen, especially with the view he has from his living room. I ask him how many steelhead he has caught in the lie below the house and he shrugs and says, "Oh gosh, I haven't kept count but I've caught several in that spot."

I ask him if it has a name. "I don't know what others call it, but I call it the "Drowning Hole." It starts out shallow and when you get out to your waist the current is such that you can't turn around and go back. The first time I fished it I had to swim back to shore."

Background

Keith: My dad's boss taught me to fly-cast on the Middle Fork of the Clearwater when I was seven. He had a cabin up there by Three Rivers and he taught me how to fly-cast, all the wrong ways of course, with a book tucked under my arm. Eventually I managed to break all those bad habits, but it took me forty years to do it.

The first recollection I have of steelhead is in 1956 when I was a sophomore in high school. We were camping on the North Fork on Labor Day in the Black Canyon at the Cedars Campground. I was fly-fishing for cutthroat. I saw this enormous fish come up to the surface a few times and I spent a long time that afternoon changing flies in an attempt to catch it. Finally, I tied on a Fantail Royal Coachman that had a tendency to twitter a lot in the water and that 12-15-pound steelhead took it. I didn't have it on for very long, but it was sure exciting. I realized then that I had hooked one of those North Fork steelhead.

I started fly-fishing for steelhead on the Clearwater in 1964 after I completed college. I still remember my first steelhead on a fly, that's one you always remember. I was fishing at Spalding near the bridge. In those days the only people that were fishing for steelhead were the few little boats that putted around the Lewiston city limits and a cadre of people that fished off the Spalding Bridge, but none of them were fly-fishermen.

One crisp, cool fall evening, for whatever reason, I put on a Fall Favorite. In those days we were using sinking lines and I hooked this crazy hen above the bridge. The fish was in an awful panic running all over the river and I thought it was going to wrap around the center post of the bridge, but I was able to apply enough pressure to make it turn, not knowing what I was doing and for whatever reason that worked. One of the conservation officers saw this going on and he came running down the bank as excited as I was. He kept ordering me not to lose the fish. I finally landed it, it was a nice wild hen about 12 pounds.

That was in 1964 and that experience got me feel pretty well sold on the idea of catching steelhead on a fly. It was quite a while before I caught my second fish, but I knew then that I had to find out something about this sport. Back then the only fly-fishermen were some California fellows. A lot of them had found out about the Clearwater on their motor-home trips to British Columbia. They would stop here on their way and fish. After a while a lot of them just started staying here because they figured the fishing here was better than up in the Skeena River drainage."

I think that Bob Weddell and I were the first local anglers to start greased-line fishing at about the same time. We observed a couple of fellows from the Seattle area (Walt Price, Bill Nelson) fishing with floating lines on the Grande Ronde in the mid 60s and we couldn't figure out what in the world they were doing, fishing a Muddler and absolutely slaying the fish. It was amazing how many steelhead they released in a day.

It was a combination of watching those men fish and reading some of the old English literature on greased lines and Atlantic salmon. I figured if the method would work for Atlantic salmon there was no reason it shouldn't work for steelhead, and it did.

Bomber dry fly patterns are some of Keith Stonebraker's favorites.

Pink Bomber
(tied by LeRoy Hyatt)

Tail: Deer hair
Body: Spun deer hair
Wing: Deer body hair or white calf tail

The first fish I caught on the surface was across from Potlatch in 1967 when it was a free-flowing stretch, pre-Dworshak days.

We started using damp flies beneath the surface, skating patterns, Bombers and that sort of thing. I learned a long time ago that it really doesn't make much difference what pattern you use. I do think that the small flies are better, especially wet flies. Most of my fish have been caught on sixes and eights and the last few years and I have started using twelves. They actually worked quite well.

Sometimes the fish will play with a skating fly. I have seen them come up and whack it with their tail. It's like they are trying to drown it first then they come back. I've had them hit it with their tail, flop over it and then circle around and hit it. If a fish is playing with a skating pattern then I switch to a smaller fly, preferably a size 12.

I like a Bomber tied so that I can put a riffle hitch on it. One of my favorite Bombers is a size 8 yellow deer-hair body with a white tail tied by LeRoy Hyatt. I mostly use two different rods, and sometimes I use one of my bamboo rods but not very often. If it looks like wind I use an 8 weight 10-foot, but my favorite rod is a 6 weight 10-foot rod that Tom Morgan from the Winston Rod Company built me. It's the same rod I use in a float tube. Tom lived in Clarkston for a few years and he was a fine fisherman. I told Steve Pettit that if he ever sees me on the river with a two-handed rod he has permission to shoot me.

Floating lines still work when the water temperature is down in the 30s, but only if the temperature has dropped recently say from 44 degrees down to 38. But within 2-3 weeks the fishes' metabolism slows down to where they aren't as aggressive going after a fly, at these times I will sometimes switch to a sink-tip. Steelhead fishing is a matter of pounding the water and working at it as long as you can. If I have a run to myself I usually fish it again a second time, especially if it is at a place where I have caught fish before. I fish at a moderate speed and just take a couple of steps between casts. When I feel a strike, I just tighten up and let the fish go.

I'm a great one for switching patterns if I've felt a grab. I will usually switch to something really small like a size twelve. I am more concerned about the size than the color. I don't think color makes that much difference. Sometimes I think they will hammer a small speck compared to a big fly, a lot of times they will play with a larger fly. They tend to engulf a small speck and it really seems to work. I've caught several of the large B-runs on size 12's. The biggest B-run fish I ever took on a fly was 22 1/2 pounds 42 inches long on a Fall Favorite.

I was on a river on the west coast this year and was using a size eight. The fish just kept barely pecking at it, peck, peck, peck...so I switched to a little double-hook size 12 that I had picked up in Scotland, they were small Silver Doctors and, boy, did that work. The next cast I caught a 15 lb hen, it was a beautiful fish, out of the water more than it was in and the hook held, but after about 5 or 6 fish one of the hooks broke off. I've since used those patterns around here and they work well.

We all have these stories where a fish keeps coming to a fly. Several years ago I had a fish come up to the darn fly at least 14 times before he took on the 15th. I was switching flies the whole time, I kept getting smaller and smaller and he finally inhaled a size 10. That was exciting but I was about ready to go out of my mind. That's exciting when you see the boil and a fish working on it.

Then there are those other fish that show one time and that's it. I don't know whether they go to a different station or what. Sometimes I shorten the line or extend it, I might walk down a couple of feet and occasionally you can take the fish above or below where they were the first time. I've had that happen quite a bit.

Dworshak

Dworshak is a project that should have never been built. It would never be approved today because the cost-benefit ratio wouldn't be good enough. At that time the Corps of Engineers was working on Dworshak and Lower Granite. They came into here with the most incredible public relations ploys that you ever heard. They brought in some guy right out of the Pentagon, a brigadier general from Washington, and he told the Lewiston Chamber of Commerce that these turbines are so safe for fish, he said, "That you could throw a horse through these turbines and he would come up whole if he didn't drown first."

I was there when he said that. Some one from the audience asked him about the horror stories they had heard about how these turbines chop up fish. "Oh no, you could throw a horse in there and he would come up whole on the other side if it didn't drown," the general replied.

The chamber manager was so convinced by what he heard from the Corps that he was telling everyone that Lewiston would soon have a population of 150,000 and that the dams would be a real boon to the region. Lewiston would soon have more people and be the hub of the inland empire and have more economic development than Spokane. It was going to be curtains for Spokane and accolades for Lewiston. Boy, I tell you the Corp did a heck of a job. Just think how good the fishing would be today if those predictions had come true. Growth does have its down side.

Mel Leven

Mel Leven, from Walt Disney studios, started fishing the Grande Ronde and Clearwater in the 1960s.

Mel Leven is one of the original anglers from the Walt Disney studios that started fishing the Grande Ronde and Clearwater in the early 1960s. Mel was one of the principal producers of the animated Disney film "101 Dalmatians" and was the voice in many of the Disney commercials. Mel was a good friend of Ted Trueblood and Jimmy Green who he fished with in California on the Russian River and on the Grande Ronde. Mel was friends with Ed Ward, Ken Petersen, Ken Anderson, Duke Parkening, Terry Glykening, and Milt Kahl. Mel has been an avid fisherman all his life and has fished all over the world.

Mel: I first started fishing the Salmon River in the 1950s. It was fly-fishing only and I fished High D lines. Ted Trueblood showed the Ronde to my friend Jimmy Green. Ted wrote about the river but he just called it the unnamed river.

I fished a lot with my friend Terry Glykening. Terry worked at Disney and wrote "Pride of the Wild Goose." We showed up there every year at Halloween. We fished the Grande Ronde and Snake for a couple days and then headed for the Clearwater. Some years it was warm and you could fish in shirt sleeves and other times it was cold and snowing.

I was good friends of Bill Schaadt and Bob Weddell. I fished with Bob in the early years. Bob Weddell is a great fisherman and

Boss
(tied by Mel Leven)

Tail: Black bucktail
Body: Black with silver tinsel ribbing
Hackle: Red
Head: Silver bead chain eyes

The Boss in small sizes was one of Mel's favorite flies.

he was a fishing partner of Bill Schaadt. One of the last times I fished with Bob he was ahead of me and I caught a 12-pound fish on a dry. He had raised the fish first and then moved on down.

I fished the North Fork a long ways up in the 1960s. We did not go as far as Kelly Creek but we went a long ways on an old dirt road. I can remember seeing large trout up to 24 inches in the North Fork, but we passed them up because we were after steelhead. I'm sorry I passed that up, I love to trout fish. I always thought the North Fork fish had a lot of color, were a very beautiful fish, and surprisingly solid after traveling so far.

Compared to all the steelhead rivers I have fished, I rate the North Fork as the greatest of all. The Russian River was good before they put in a dam but the scenery on the North Fork is great. Also, it was better fishing and few people. You could catch a fish behind every rock, any hole, anywhere on the river was good. The North Fork fish fought just as well as fish in other rivers.

Dworshak just killed us. Because of Dworshak, the steelheading was shot to hell. It was just terrible, terrible because they didn't have a fish ladder. It made me sick when I heard people bragging about the bluegill and bass fishery on the lake that formed above the dam. Can you believe people would ruin a steelhead fishery for bluegills and bass?

The biggest fish I think I ever caught on the Clearwater was an 18-20-pound fish that was 40 inches. I had a lot of 40-plus-inch fish on but didn't land them. There was one run on the Clearwater where I could count on catching at least three fish that would go 15 pounds. After I caught the third fish I would leave and not come back till the next day and catch another three.

I always fished wet flies in the early years and didn't start using dry flies till later on. I fished using the greased-line method and it was great to get those grabs as the fly was sweeping across. A great fly at times was an adult Montana Stone Fly. My favorite flies were the original Skunk, the Golden Demon, and my own pattern which I call an Orange Bastard. It is a fly that has no body but consists of palmered red hackle in front, orange hackle then yellow hackle, unweighted. It kind of looks like a Woolly Worm. Sometimes I fish a Skunk with a white wing and I use white hackle at the head with a black body and silver tinsel and a red tail. The last few years I have used a Boss that has a bead-chain eye, black body, tinsel rib, orange hackle and black tail.

I have a story about fishing with Duke Parkening. We were fishing together at the run above the Cherry Lane Bridge on the Clearwater. Duke was in front of me and as we were getting close to the bridge Duke started to get out. I told him not to quit because I had seen some fish down below him and they looked big.

He said he was going to quit anyway and got out and was standing on the bank. I kept on fishing and I hit one of the biggest fish ever, easily a plus 20 pounder. Duke got sore and started yelling. I told him, "You dumb bastard, don't get sore I told you not to get out of the water."

Well, the fish finally went under a rock and broke off but Duke always maintained that I went in front of him and cut him off. Even when we see each other today after all those years, that still comes up. I like to give him a hard time about it because he knows that I would never cut anyone off or go in front of them, that's not something I would ever do. It's still fun to bring up that story when I see him.

Asotin Creek Canyon.

1970s

Dicksie House of Walla Walla caught this 14-pound Clearwater fish on a Max Canyon Fly in 1986.

Gale House, who has lived in Walla Walla since the 1960s, has fished the Clearwater since 1970. He also fished the Grande Ronde near Troy, Oregon in 1966 and remembers taking some fine fish from that area. In 1967 he met Tom Morgan in Ennis, Montana and through Tom he became friends with Keith Stonebraker and Doug Venerka.

Gale is a good photographer and he also wrote a Clearwater steelheading article that was published in the 1995 winter issue of Frank Amato's *Steelhead Fly-fishing Journal.* Gale and his wife Dicksie were married in 1980 and Dicksie fished the Ronde and Clearwater for almost ten years.

Background

Gale: I started fly-fishing when I returned home after the war from flying over in England. I moved to Walla Walla after the war and took a job as a district engineer for Pacific Power and Light. I organized a brand-new John Deer dealership here in October of 1959.

I sold the dealership in 1964 and started an investment business and that's when I had a lot more time to fish. In 1966 we started fly-fishing the Grande Ronde. On that first trip a fellow by the name of Ed Zaring took us to the river. We went up there, put on an old scraggly fly and cast it out and caught a few fish.

In 1970 I met Keith Stonebraker because of my association with Tom Morgan. I had first met and heard of Tom in 1966-67

Gale and Dicksie House

when I was fishing the Madison River in Montana and stayed at the El Western Motel in Ennis Montana. Anyway, I met Keith Stonebraker and Tom Morgan at a coffee shop in Clarkston and we visited for a couple of hours, exploring and talking about greased-line fishing.

Dicksie and I were married in 1980. She had never fished, never held a fly rod in her hand. Tom Morgan gave her a fly rod for a wedding present and we started fishing in Montana. Her first steelhead fishing was in the fall of 1980. I bought her a steelhead rod and she fished for almost ten years.

Dicksie: My first fly-fishing lesson was in the back yard and then Keith Stonebraker gave me 15 minutes worth of lessons at Winchester Lake. From then on I was pretty much on my own. I don't think I caught a steelhead that first year.

The first fish I ever caught was by an Island. You have to wade way across. In fact, Gale took me out about knee deep and he told me to keep going across. Anyway, I proceeded across to the island and that's where I caught my first fish.

I don't have the passion for steelhead fishing that Gale does and I don't pretend that I do. My biggest enjoyment was being in the outdoors, looking around at the absolutely fabulous countryside. The kick of course is getting one of those things on. I know I broke off more than I ever landed. When you know you have one on there is a rush that you can't deny.

I had the patience to fish for them. I did all five thousand casts just like everyone else. Gale always put me in the run first, which is the gentlemanly thing to do, so I would have first crack at a fish. I would fish down through the run and of course I would always hear from Gale, "Wade a little deeper, dear." You know, the classic instructions.

My favorite pattern was a Max Canyon. I tried Green Butt Skunks and Princeton Tigers, but I always seemed to have the best luck with a Max Canyon. Those were the three patterns I used the most.

Gale: We always fished using the greased-line method and those years in the 1970s were great times because there was very little boat traffic. Most steelhead fishermen will tell you that the pattern is not all that important but nevertheless we all have our favorites. Some of mine include an Orange Shrimp Spey, Silver Doctor, Princeton Tiger, and the Mudstut Special. Other favorites include an assortment of Spey flies in red, black, purple, blue, and chartreuse.

The Mudstut Special is my favorite dry fly that is an adaptation of a Muddler with a gold body and some flash with a spun head that aids it riding the surface in a waking action. I used it first on the Sustut River in British Columbia and thereupon called it a Mudstut Special. It is an excellent locator and if it is just "boiled" with no take, I change to a damp Spey pattern and put it back in the same drift usually with great results.

For several years I used that Princeton Tiger that Ed Ward had showed me almost exclusively. Al Bradford didn't fish anything else. If he couldn't get a fish to take a Princeton Tiger he figured the fish weren't taking.

Somewhere along the line I became enthused with the Spey patterns. The reason being is that as you see them in the water there is that breathing animated action. I just gravitated towards them because first of all they are very pretty and appealing to the eye and I started using them in conjunction with a waking fly. I found that in most instances, on days that were suitable and on

Gale House of Walla Walla with a Clearwater steelhead.

runs that were suitable for fishing a dry or waking fly, that I used that as a locater.

I became more comfortable with using the dry or waking fly as a locater and if I could locate the fish then I knew exactly where he was. Then I would switch to a damp Spey fly. I felt that I could get 85 or 90 percent success rate with that technique. A number of the bigger fish I have taken were caught that way.

The last 10 or 15 years I don't think I've tied anything other than a down-eyed number six for a waking fly and a number three Alex Jackson Spey hook for the wet flies. Most of my Speys that have no name are adaptations of Alex Jackson Speys. He used a combination of Japanese silk wound with small gold wire and then you tie on some seal fur.

Clearwater Story

In October of 1972 I met Ed Ward and Milt Kahl on the river one evening. They were just leaving a run on the lower river and I could see them coming out. We stopped to talk and they told me they hadn't done anything.

Ed Ward asked me, "Had I ever used this fly?" and he gave me a Princeton Tiger.

I said, "No, I've never seen it before."

He said, "It's a good fly."

I didn't use it that evening but I do remember that I was using 2x Maxima. I don't think I made over one cast when I got there that I didn't raise a fish and here Ed Ward hadn't done anything. I'm sure that those fish had moved in there while we had been talking. That whole run was alive with fish. I proceeded to hook seven fish in a row and all of them broke off. They would take me downstream, break off, I would go back up, put another fly on, replace the tippet and go back down through there and immediately hook another fish.

I don't think I had a single cast that didn't raise a fish. Finally when it was dark I landed the last fish, about 7:00. I killed the fish because I had some people coming for a barbecue and I wanted to grill it.

I was staying with Keith that night and so I went to his home and he suggested that we take it down to a butcher shop, so we did and it weighed 18 pounds. That was a Friday night. Keith and I went back there Saturday morning, real early. I think Keith took a small fish that was maybe five or six pounds and that was it. They were gone. It was just one of those unbelievable evenings.

Memorable Fish

The biggest fish I ever caught on the Clearwater began one evening with Al Bradford. We were fishing where the casino now is. There's a little curl there that everyone fishes because it runs out there a long way and you can cover an awful lot of water. There is a gravel bar that extends up river from there, so you wade right upstream and you can fish that dead water that sort of pushes against that jetty and then starts to spill out.

I had a small dry on about a number 10. It was just chattering along out there and I rose this fish three or four times. It was a big fish. There was no question about it. I could see the dorsal fin and the tail come out of the water. Well, it got dark, absolutely dark, so that was the end of it. It didn't raise every time. I tried switching flies a few times, I bet I spent at least a half hour with him.

So anyway, I thought he still might be there the next morning. So first thing in the morning, there we were. Al started fishing down below the break and I waded back up river. I put on a Spey fly and I kept working down, working down and all a of sudden there he was. We fiddled around out there in that big deep water. I knew he was big, no head shake, nothing.

I'm carefully wading, trying to get myself back to the bank. I had about 75 feet to get to the bank. All of sudden he decides to take off and ended up lodging himself out in the middle of the river. I got out on the bank and walked down. I stood next to the bank and applied side pressure. I would gain a few feet and then he would go back behind some big rocks. We did this for a whole hour of just tug-of-war. I would pull him out and he would go back, pull him out and he would go back.

He had absolutely no desire to run downstream or anything. He never jumped or ever showed himself at all. I don't think he knew he was even hooked. One hour after that, I finally landed him. I had a little tape measure with me, I handed it to Al but it wasn't long enough. So I laid my fly rod alongside of him and marked the rod from the second uppermost guide to a spot on the cork. I told Al we would measure it when we got back up to the car.

Anyway when we got back up to the car, lo and behold there is an Idaho State game official. He said, "I saw you land that fish, how big was he?"

I said, "I don't know, it was a big fish, but I have the measurements here on the rod. Well, he had a tape measure in his rig and it measured 44 1/4 inches.

Of course the Clearwater fish don't have very big girths. A 44-inch fish on the Babine will weigh 35 pounds. I landed a 40-inch fish with a 24-inch girth up there that weighed 30 pounds and it took a dry. That probably is the epitome of steelhead fishing.

Another Memorable Clearwater Fish

The one fish I remember the most was when Al and I were fishing near Myrtle. At that time the steel bridge was still there but they were getting ready to remove it. You couldn't drive a vehicle across it but you could walk across it. I started fishing there one morning. I rose this fish three or four times and he finally took. He was absolutely oblivious to what was happening, defiant.

He took and then swam immediately into the shallow water and then he came right up to me and I could have almost touched him. All this time I was hollering at him, go away, go away, because I have a full reel of line that is slack and the fish is fresh and I knew what was going to happen. The minute that he took off he would bust everything.

I got a good look at him and he was a big fish. Well, he finally saw me and bolted. The next thing I find is that I'm hung up. I can't feel him anymore because I'm hung up in the rocks. He

The Princeton Tiger was another favorite of Gale and Dicksie House that was also fished a lot by Ed Ward.

Princeton Tiger
(tied by Gale House)

Body: Black with silver tinsel ribbing
Wing: Orange calf or bucktail
Hackle: Black

Gale and Dicksie House had several favorite patterns including Gale's own Mudstut Special.

Mudstut Special
(tied by Gale House)

Body: Gold body
Wing: Bucktail with some flash material
Head: Spun deer hair

had just weaved himself through a whole bunch of boulders and just lined me. There was only one thing I could do. I went back around, you can't wade across there because it's too deep. You have to go back up and wade along the bank and then finally down below there you can wade out quite a long ways into the river.

I finally got out there and all of a sudden I've got my fly line loose. Lo and behold the fish was still on. Holy cow! Well, the minute I started putting some pressure on him he turned and bolts downstream and repeats the same process all over again. He lined me again. I worked for a long time, finally got the line loose and he went farther downstream. By now two hours have went by and he lines me again.

There is no possible way to get below him and free the line up. All of a sudden a troop of Boy Scouts came canoeing down the river. I hollered at the troop leader to come over. He came over and I asked him to take my fly rod out and paddle out in the river and see if he could free up the line. By that time there was about 150 yards of backing between me and the line. All I wanted now was my fly line back.

So he paddled out there and wiggled the rod and came back with the rod and said the fish is still on. Well, all he was feeling was the current against the line. So it was left to me to do nothing but wade out as far as I could and start retrieving line. Finally the line broke and I ended up leaving about 100 yards of backing and line out in the river. I lost everything! Two hours of that, Dang!

He was one of those typical big fish that are almost immune to being hooked. Those big fish are altogether different.

Steve Pettit

When one starts talking about fly-fishing for steelhead in the Lewiston area, Steve Pettit's name is always mentioned. Steve has a unique perspective when it comes to steelhead in that he has worked with steelhead for over 30 years as a fisheries biologist for the Idaho Fish and Game and he is an avid fly-fisherman. He has also spent a lot of time scuba diving the local rivers so his knowledge of steelhead biology and the associated politics is second to none.

Keith Stonebraker had this to say about Steve: "Steve Pettit came along in the early 70s. He was a fish biologist and has refused to go anyplace else. He could have been head of the department in Boise had he wanted. He is a fine biologist, I don't know what's going to happen after he retires because he is one of the few that will walk into harm's way and he's not afraid of expressing his opinion. Politically, you're not supposed to do that. That's the reason I think the world of Steve, he has enough guts to stand up for what is right and he's not going to play footsie with the guys in the black hats. I think it's great that we have him and I am going to rue the day when he retires.

He takes long periods of time to go fishing. He will take 30 day's leave fishing. I have never seen anything like it, I have never seen anyone fish harder. My gosh, he will get up at 3:00 in the morning for 30 straight days and he will be on the water till dark each day. He really works at it. If I did that for one week, I would be ready for the rubber room."

At the time of this interview in the fall of 2002, Steve was ten months away from retirement and already had plans to stay involved in activities that will help the species survive.

Background

Steve: I came to Idaho as a graduate student in the fall of 1970. I started a program in zoology with an emphasis on ichthyology and fisheries under Dick Wallace, my major professor. Starting that first summer I went to work for the cooperative fishery unit and ran the Kelly Creek cutthroat catch-and-release project for two summers in '71 and '72.

In the fall of 1970 one of my fellow graduate students, who is also a fish and game employee now, Dick Scully and Lewiston resident, took me down steelhead fishing on the Clearwater with a spinning rod in early October that year. We caught a couple fish. By the first of November I had had several fish hit the spoon as it was coming through the riffles on the surface and I said, you know, if they will come up and eat the spoon on the surface as it's skipping across the waves as I'm retrieving it in shallow water in the riffle, then I can catch these things on a fly.

So then with the crudest fly-fishing equipment one could imagine, an old Eagle Claw 7-weight glass rod and a Pflueger Medalist reel and a floating line, I came down here and I lost like 15 fish in a row before I landed one. It was on about the 15th of November that fall. It was totally addictive.

The second year of my graduate studies up at the university I purposely scheduled my classes so I would have one complete day and one afternoon free so I could come down and fish. I think it was early in that fall that I gave Keith Stonebraker a call. Somebody had given me his name, someone who knew about steelhead fly-fishing. I made contact with Keith and picked his brain a little bit.

I finished up my thesis in late winter of '72 and the Fish and Game Department hired me in the spring of 1973. I moved to Lewiston as one of the two biologists assigned to the Dworshak Reservoir Dam Project that the Corp funded for five years. That project entailed studying the reservoir fishery itself, the North Fork above the reservoir, and the impact of the reservoir on the lower Clearwater River.

I was assigned that lower Clearwater slot, so I became the de facto Clearwater steelhead biologist. I did that through the '70s. After the Dworshak investigations were over in 1978 I continued working with steelhead. I did a lot of behavior, catch-and-release mortality research with telemetry techniques. In 1980 it became apparent that the big bottleneck to the steelhead and salmon runs in Idaho was the hydro system and at that point in time the chief of fisheries came to me and said that he would like to reassign me from a research biologist to a management type of position.

They were going to create this special slot and give me a title of Idaho's Fish Passage Specialist. They just threw me into that mainstem passage arena as green as anybody could be and for the last 20 years of my career that's what I've done. I've played bio-politics with the mainstem hydro system and I will be retiring in 10 months.

The first 25 years were great, but the Idaho politics has more or less turned anti-fish in my opinion and I'm totally frustrated. I go to all the committees and working groups that I represent the State on at the technical level and make the best call based on my 30 years of main-stem passage knowledge to improve the plight of our anadromous species, only to have that reversed at the next higher level.

I had the sense when I was working under the Andrus years that the natural resources of the state were just as important as any other resource in the state. Once that regime changed and governor Batt came on, followed by Governor Kempthorne, I just don't have that same feeling. I don't think that natural resources are number one or even equal to the other resources in the state. If we are going to save Snake River salmon and steelhead that parity has to return, in my opinion, or the fish are doomed. I, quite frankly, feel that right now I can probably be a better advocate for Idaho's salmon and steelhead as a civilian rather than a Fish and Game employee.

The first year that I was a Fish and Game employee we had a pretty good return of steelhead in 1973, but early on in 1974 based on the Bonneville Dam count, it became quickly apparent that the survival of migrating steelhead was going to be astoundingly poor, lower than anybody in 50 years could remember. In fact, I think the total count at Ice Harbor that year ended up being less than 6000 fish. So, right off the bat, the first week of October we canceled the steelhead season and there was no consumptive or non-consumptive fishery in the fall of 1974.

What had happened was that in an attempt to reduce total gas super-saturation problems at the Snake River dams, which at that point in time in 1971 they only had half the turbines in the powerhouse. Instead of having six spinning units during the highwater runoff, each powerhouse only had half the capacity of the dams that were constructed that is, and they had to spill a greater volume of water, and to try to alleviate that they put these slotted bulkheads down into the turbine bays to try to reduce, to allow water to go through the dam rather than spill all of it. What

Kelly Creek, a tributary of the North Fork River, historically was a spawning stream for both salmon and steelhead.

it did was grind up fish into fish meal. That was the main thing that was responsible for that very, very poor run in 1974.

In 1975, I did a research project by clipping and releasing fish. We got quite a few of those fish back at the Dworshak Fish Hatchery, enough to allow me to make a presentation to the Game and Fish Commission to propose during these very lean years that we were going to experience like 1974 for a non-con-

sumptive steelhead fishery. That went over with the local fishing population like a lead balloon.

I was requested by one of the commissioners to have me do a full-blown catch-and-release study. So that was worked into my job description. In 1976-77 we tagged a couple hundred adult hatchery steelhead each fall and those fish were sorted out of the hatchery rack because they had jaw tags on them. They were spawned in a controlled experiment with fish that came back that hadn't been caught and released.

The critics to catch and release all through the region from Orofino to Lewiston said that even though a fish might swim away after it was released, that it was doomed and would never be able to spawn successfully because of the stresses of being caught and released.

My study went out to prove or disprove that. That study was published in the journals of the American Fisheries Society and we found that there was no significant difference between played and unplayed female eye-up success, and, in fact, even though it wasn't statistically significant the fish that had been played had a percentage point or two higher eye-up success than the fish that returned to the hatchery that hadn't been caught and released.

It was a very high eye-up success which is how you measure viability of any given female's spawning success. It was up near 90% eye-up success, so armed with that information, the Commission enacted a couple of catch-and-release years in the mid 70s. 1976 was a catch-and-release year, then we had a big return in 1977 and then the following year in 1978 was miserable so that was a non-consumptive year.

In 1979 we had another consumptive fishery. 1978 was the last year we had catch-and-release only. In 1975 it was a catch-and-release season from September 1 to December 31. In 78, the same thing. We didn't want to harass these fish past the first of the year when the eggs are starting to mature, so that year we had a fall season only.

Then we realized that the wild stocks in the Clearwater River were going downhill at a frightening pace, based on adult returns. We also knew that the earliest-arriving fish to the Clearwate, which used to be a hell of a lot different than it is now, by the way. This river was full of fish in the '70s and early '80s by October 1st. My birthday is in mid September and it was a tradition for me to go out and catch a couple of B run sized Clearwater fish in mid September without any problem. That's certainly not the case any longer.

We realized that the earliest returning fish in September and early October were mostly wild fish. Somewhere in the early 80s we developed a regulation that would make the first two weeks of October catch and release to try and allow as many of those wild fish to go through the fishery before the bulk of the hatchery fish arrived. That was the biological impetus for that regulation.

In the late '80s and early '90s there was a lot of pressure by the river guides to do away with that. There were several major battles and hearings held to defend that two-week catch-and-release season. They wanted to start killing fish the first of October. Burt Boler was the regional fisheries manager at that time and he, along with Commissioner Stonebraker and myself, presented an argument that the regulation was not just to provide safe passage for those early-arriving wild fish, but it had also become a very strong social regulation and that the Clearwater River was such a famous steelhead stream that it ought to afford an opportunity to all types of fishing.

If the aluminum hatch were to start October 1st it was going to really cut into the opportunity of fly-fishermen that came from all around the world to fish the river. The Commission bought that and it has been the regulation ever since. Because of people jumping the gun, the non-consumptive fishery was officially moved back to September 1 in the late 1980s or early '90s.

There was quite a controversy about whether or not anglers could say they were just catch-and-release fishing when the season hadn't officially opened. I think the Department just didn't want to deal with it after having unsuccessful attempts to write tickets to the magistrates around here, so they just said okay, you can start steelhead fishing September 1 but it is going to be a six-week non-consumptive fishery instead of two weeks. Many fishermen start steelheading around here in June. The boats are even out in force but they tend to concentrate in the lower river.

Behavior and Timing of B-run Steelhead

In the 30 years that I have been associated with the Clearwater River, I've seen a huge dramatic change in life-history behavior by both the hatchery and wild B-run fish. Back in the late 60s and early 70s there was a good solid penetration into the Clearwater by B-run fish in September. By October 1st, when the season used to open, the river was full of 30-40-inch fish.

That started to change in the late '80s. The early-season fishing started getting harder and harder. It just kept getting significantly delayed year after year to where now I really don't fish the Clearwater till the second or third week of November. I just don't think there are that many B-run fish in the river. There are several theories about what is going on.

The primary reason I think is that the bulk of the fish that come back are hatchery fish. Eighty to 90% of the fish that return now are Dworshak Hatchery fish. The early-arriving fish I think has just been selected out of the gene pool. A 30-year hatchery history. Fish are very heritable organisms. Some animals it takes hundreds of years to change their behavior. With fish, on the other hand, you can see changes in only one or two generations, you can significantly change that critter.

Nothing illustrates that more than what I've been talking about. Some of the problem was hatchery oriented. The hatchery didn't open the gates to the hatchery till the first of the year in the first decade of its operation and so the earliest-returning fish were just trapped out there in the river. The longer that fish sits in the Clearwater, the longer it's subjected to fishing pressure. So year after year after year the fish that the local residents harvest the most are the first ones that get here. Plus the fact that the hatchery wasn't taking them in just added to the problem.

I was able to convince the regional supervisor to support me when I went to the Dworshak Coordination meeting representing the Department that the hatchery managers should be forced to start opening that gate in the fall months so that they could start collecting fish that had some early-arriving genes in them. They started doing that, but they didn't have a very good holding environment and they would bring 500 fish in October and November but none of them were alive by the time they spawned the fish. They died in the ponds.

They worked on that holding environment and I understand now that it's standard operating procedure for them to take a group of early-arriving fish and they do seem to make it through 2-3 months before the first fish arrive in February or March.

But more importantly, since the fish were listed under the Endangered Species Act and the cornerstone of the federal recovery plan championed by the National Marine Fisheries Service is to provide cool water for summer-migrating fall chinook juveniles in the Snake River by drastically lowering Dworshak Reservoir during the summer, to provide those cooler higher flows is necessary to improve the survival of fall chinook juveniles which migrate during the summer months. That biological opinion in the recovery plan requires the reservoir to be drafted 80 feet by September 1st. In the old days the way they would operate that reservoir was to keep it at full pool all summer long for recreation and log drives.

The first 23 years of its operation, that's how it was operated. On September 1 they would begin a 30-day temporary draft of the reservoir to do one thing, to lower the reservoir low enough so they could hold the flows at minimum discharge for steelhead fishing starting October 1 through November 15. The only way they could do that was to create a 25-30-foot hole in the reservoir so that the natural inflow for that first six weeks of the old historic steelhead season on October 1, we called it the prime steelhead fishing weeks, that six week period when the weather is nice and everybody likes to go fishing, from Octtober 1 to mid November.

There was only 1300 cfs above inflow allowed to come out of that powerhouse. If we had a really wet fall, the only way they could guarantee that to happen was to release a powerhouse capacity discharge of cold water from September 1-30. It sucked for fly-fishing, but it was very very influential for sucking a bunch of B-run steelhead into the Clearwater early. So when the flows dropped back to normal on October 1 there had been a month of high fish passage into the Clearwater because of that high, cool water.

That stopped in 1993 and it's been operated the way it is now, jumping the water in the summertime because it's high and 46 degrees. That doesn't help the B-run fish because the B-runs haven't even come across Bonneville yet, (but it's been phenomenal.) That's why everyone is fishing now is because the Snake River is 70-73 degrees which is semi lethal for a salmonid and the Clearwater is 58 at the confluence so any self-respecting steelhead that is migrating up the Snake River and has already crossed Lower Granite pulls into the lower Clearwater. Ninety-nine percent of those fish aren't Clearwater stocked fish and they are the smaller fish.

Some of the fish that are around 30 inches are probably two-salt A fish. So the combination of selecting the earliest-arriving fish out of the population because they're subjected to fishing pressure the longest for years, that early arriving gene is just gone. I think it is actually extinct. Then you add insult to injury with the way Dworshak is operating now because of the Endangered Species Act, it just adds insult to injury because the B-run fish hit the confluence, the flows in the Clearwater are so low that it takes a major rain event that usually happens in early November for a significant pulse of B-run fish to come into the Clearwater.

If we tried to adjust the seasons and move them back to compensate we would never be able to sell that to the public. It would be great for the fly-fishermen, but it wouldn't sell.

That to me has been the biggest significant change in the river since I've been here, but it is only slightly more significant than the Skagit navy. That to me, when the Skagit River wildcat

Snake River near Asotin, Washington.

steelhead group discovered the Clearwater River ten years ago, I can remember it very vividly. A few of them came over here about ten years ago and the word just went out. The steelhead fishery in the Skagit has been a disaster for the last 20 years and those people fish hard and they came over here and discovered this fishery and it just increased exponentially, so now every jet sled from Sedro-Woolley is over every year for 4-6 weeks.

Most of them aren't guiding they are just fishing. I watch them pretty carefully, there are some crooks out there, there is some illegal guiding, no doubt, but the bulk of them are just hard serious Pacific Northwest steelhead jet boaters and they know a good deal when they see it. They haven't had any fall steelhead fishing on the Skagit for 20 years and now the winter-run steelhead fishery is so depressed that those seasons have been drastically cut or eliminated all together.

The impact of that on the wading fisherman has been huge, because the way those guys fish roaring up to the top of a pool and fishing with these noodle rods and a single egg or two, they're competing in the exact same waters that the fly-fishermen use, whereas the jet boaters pulling plugs tend to fish a little bit different part of the run. But these guys are competing for the exact same water as the wading fly-fishermen, so that and the fact of the timing behavior is the biggest thing I've seen change in 30 years.

Movement

When a steelhead is actively migrating, it migrates as fast as you can walk up the railroad tracks at a steady walk. That's how fast they go, that's the best way I can describe it. They can easily go 8-12 miles a day. Steelhead are a lot different than chinook. When chinook migrate into the Snake River they just go, they don't hold. There's no real holding phenomenon in their migration. They may rest a couple of hours, but then they just get up and go the next day. Their biological clock is ticking and they have to be in the vicinity of their spawning grounds a lot faster than steelhead do.

Steelhead migration behavior is quite a bit different. Where a steelhead can come into the Clearwater River and put its head behind a rock and stay there for 30 days because it's in no great rush to go anywhere because it's not going to spawn for 9-11 months for those first arriving fish.

Rapid changes in their environment can invoke really bizarre movements. A flood event in the Clearwater once chased a transmitter-equipped fish that was up the river right below Kooskia all the way down to Nisqually John landing near Lower Granite Dam in 24 hours. I located that fish down in the reservoir when he traveled over 60 miles in 24 hours then that same fish stayed down there for 48 hours and then I tracked it going by my house the day after it started moving upstream again.

It's amazing what they can do. Movement of over 20 miles in one day is a rare event. Steelhead, once they get in the river, they really slow down. They can set behind a rock for a week at a time and then get up and move a few miles and stay there for two months. There is a lot of inter-pool movement, fish will move back and forth from one side of the river to the other all winter long in the same run.

I've had steelhead that have stayed in the same spot for six weeks to the point I thought they were probably dead or had regurgitated the transmitter and all of a sudden on February 1 when the first water temperature rises, that fish get up and goes.

There is no mainstem spawning in the Clearwater. Steelhead just don't do it. They will attempt to spawn in the North Fork because that's a last ditch effort. If a fish hasn't gotten into the hatchery by the first of May it may try to spawn. They have a trap at the base of Dworshak Dam which they used to operate for the first 15 years of its existence. In many years they would take most of their fish from that trap at the dam and then truck them down to the hatchery.

The prevailing scientific evidence is that the lower Clearwater tributaries, say from Lolo Creek down stream, have some remnant wild fish in those tributaries but they're not B-run fish, they are A-run fish, small 24-25-inch fish. Which kind of follows the definition character of desert steelhead that spawn in ephemeral streams that have a lot of water in them in March and April but by mid-summer are almost dry.

Very few fish survive to come back and spawn more than one time. Historically, the limited information that we have is from one thesis that was done in the Clearwater River by a guy named Whitt in the 50s and he found by reading scales taken from the Washington Water Power Dam before it was removed some 500 fish two years in a row that the spawning checks of those scales indicated that less than 1.5% fish were repeat spawners. Recently a biologist for the tribe thinks that the number is actually higher based on some research from tag returns. I'm still kind of a skeptic but I think he's doing good work and if we're wrong we're wrong, but even though he is reporting repeated spawning incidents it's still not a very high number, it's 4% instead of 1%.

That's normally the case on big inland runs of summer steelhead, they have a very low repeat spawning success because of the arduous journey they have to make. Winter-run steelhead on the coast have quite high rates of repeat spawning and multiple spawning. Some can spawn 5-7 times, but those fish can come across the bar and in one day be on the spawning grounds, spawn and they go back to the ocean, so the energy demand is much lower.

Big Fish

I had been fishing the lower Clearwater River and I knew there was a large fish in the run I was fishing. I knew he was a brute. Finally after 30 minutes of casting to him one afternoon, he took the fly. It took me two hours and ten minutes to finally land that fish. I ended up going downstream at least 1/2 mile, and one time I had to climb up the bank to the road and hold the rod high above my head so the line could get around a large, partially submerged rock.

After the first hour there were about 10 cars that pulled off the road so they could get out and watch. It finally got to the point where the river was going to split around an island and he started to move out into the main current. I knew if he got out too far it was all over. I decided to take a stand and if I lost him so be it. I only had 8-pound-test leader so I was in no position to horse him around. He finally started to swing towards the shore and when he got in shallow water he couldn't swim anymore. It was a wild fish and his adipose fin was the size of a silver dollar. He measured forty-six inches and I have no idea how much he actually weighed but I'm pretty sure it was over 30 pounds. You don't see those large wild B-run fish anymore; they just aren't there anymore.

Dale Knoche

Dale Knoche (left) and long-time friend Jimmy Green in 2001, next to the Grande Ronde River.

Dale Knoche is a long-time friend of Jimmy Green and has a home along the banks of the Grande Ronde. Dale tells the following story.

Old Green Rag Story

I used to pick up Jimmy and take him down to the confluence of the Snake and Ronde. I would perch on one of the rocks and watch the old guys fish. If you were under sixty years old, people would make you feel ashamed for fishing water that was unofficially reserved for the elderly fly-fishermen. If an older person showed up, room would be made to accommodate them but if a younger person showed up, no water would be relinquished and they would all work in unison to make that person feel uncomfortable. That was the code of the river and that's just the way it was. If you were under sixty, you got no respect.

One evening I took Jimmy down to the run and he entered the water above two locals who were already there. They hadn't been there long when an older fisherman from Clarkston showed up who had a real hard time walking on the cobble rocks to get to the river. He wasn't very agile and I was worried that the man would not have the strength to reach the water and fight the current. The man was using a bamboo rod that had obviously seen a lot of use.

On the second cast, the man hooked into a fish and as he struggled to get it to shore I went down and asked him if he needed any assistance. The man said he could manage it himself so I went back to my rock and watched Jimmy cast his two-handed rod. The man landed the fish and reentered the water and on his third cast hooked another fish. I could see that the

man was really getting tired so I again went down to the waters' edge and asked the man if he needed help. He told me that my help would be appreciated so then I had the chance to see what fly pattern the man was using.

I looked at the fly in amazement and asked the man what the heck kind of a pattern was it. The man replied, "That's an Old Green Rag, it's just a piece of material from an old green wool shirt." The fly had a very short tail and the shank had been wrapped with the green material and tied off. It was the ugliest, most nondescript fly I ever laid eyes on. The man told me that he had caught hundreds of steelhead with that fly and said it is the only fly he ever used.

About that time Jimmy hooked a fish and I went over to help him land it. Jimmy asked me what pattern the man was using and I just shook my head and said you wouldn't believe it if I told you. When I started to explain to Jimmy about the Old Green Rag, the old man hooked another fish and immediately asked me for some help. He told me, that he was "all gived out" and could use the help. After he landed the fish, he left and none of us have seen him since.

People who are familiar with the story, and the group that witnessed the events of that evening, now only have one thing to say when others ask them what pattern they are using. Just an Old Green Rag, they reply, and they all have a good laugh.

Kelly Creek at one time was a traditional salmon and steelhead fishery of the Nez Perce.

Craig Lannigan

Craig Lannigan from Lewiston, Idaho is considered by many to be one of the area's finest steelhead fly-fishermen.

Craig Lannigan is one of the valley's premier steelhead fly-fishermen. He has fished the Clearwater avidly since 1972 and was one of the first fly-fisherman in the area to start using a two-handed rod. He is a school teacher in Lewiston and has taught many young people how to tie flies in the clinics he has participated in. Craig also ties salmon flies and loves to use traditional materials.

At this point in his life, Craig prefers to catch steelhead on the surface which is typified in his own words.

"Here's what I think about steelhead fishing. Only one in a thousand fly-fishermen will ever catch a steelhead on a fly, out of those, only one in a thousand will catch a steelhead on a dry fly, only one in a thousand of those will catch one on a dry fly, floating line and two-handed rod, and if you want to take it one step farther, only one in a thousand of those guys will ever catch one dead drifting a small dry. That's what I try to do."

Craig: I saw my first Idaho steelhead being cleaned in the Lewiston Orchards. My eyes couldn't believe the 16-pound male. I think I was hooked right there. I was an avid bird hunter

and one thing led to another and I started tying flies and fly-fishing. I still have the very first fly I tied that I caught a fish on, and I still have the first fly that I caught a steelhead on. It is called Craig's Ugly and it is pretty bad. It does have some polar bear in it and green and all kinds of colors, but I was never so proud of that first steelhead I caught. That was about 1972 when I caught my first steelhead.

When I first came here I learned about steelheading mostly on my own, but I did talk to Keith Stonebraker on several occasions. When I first came here I was using full-sink lines. I used to use egg patterns on the bottom. Keith was the first one to tell me to use a floating line. In that respect, I had a hard time believing you could catch a steelhead on a floating line. He told me to use a plain Muddler. I went out and tried it with a Spruce fly. I used to fish a lot of streamers.

I hooked a couple of steelhead with Spruce flies, but unfortunately I had a Berkley reel that the fish really blew the plastic gears right out of. I realized then that you could catch steelhead on a dry line and I didn't see many guys fishing a dry line at all in those days. This was in 1973-74.

My first year using flies I remember having three fish hitting the flies and losing all three. At that time I was setting the hook real hard. My second year, I hooked and landed six, I didn't try to set the hook, someone told me to just wait for the pull on the line ... which was very hard for a trout fisherman to do. The third year, I landed over a dozen. The last couple of years I've hooked close to 300 steelhead and all of them were as good as the first. I've never lost my love for these fish.

Spey Rods

The reason I switched to a Spey rod in 1988 is that it doesn't hurt my arm. I was developing bursitis and arthritis in my right shoulder, so when I would double haul a single-handed rod, I got so I couldn't cast much. It just really hurt.

I was at a fly fair and Jim Green had one of his prototype Spey rods there. I had a friend from Montana who was intrigued with it. I really wasn't interested. My friend picked that thing up and made one back cast with it and let go of it and 160 feet of line shot out with just one back cast. I went, Yow, let me look at this again. So I watched him do it some more.

I picked it up and of course I couldn't do anything with it. After that I didn't do much with it. A guy by the name of Cliff McCann came into fly-fishing for steelhead in 1985 and five years ago he just quit. He had one year where he only had three fish on, so he just quit and went back to bird hunting. I helped him get started.

Cliff and I decided that we wanted to build some Spey rods. We were actually more intrigued with building them than fishing them. We both bought the same blanks, a Sage 14 foot for a 10/11-weight line. We had no idea of what we were doing as far as knowing how to cast them. I knew how to build fly rods. We built a special press and took a long time building those first ones.

I still have mine. It was a stiff rod. We put some Cortland double-taper lines on them and I had a heck of a time casting them. One day out on the lawn, Bill Alspach said, "You're working too hard." I said, "I'm trying as hard as I can."

He said, "You're pushing too much, let the rod do it. Put half the energy into what you're doing but keep on doing, what you're doing."

Green Lantern
(tied by Dave Clark)

Tail: Squirrel tail
Body: Bright florescent green
Hackle: Match body material

The Green Lantern is one of Craig Lannigan's favorite patterns.

So I started doing that and all of a sudden the rod started loading and I could cast the thing another 30 feet with a lot less effort. Well, getting back to the arthritis. I started fishing that rod because I couldn't double haul and my idea was, well, I could get it out further, but since then I've learned that casting a two-handed rod is an art, its artwork in itself, the casting of both Spey and double Spey and the other casts. But I basically use a single Spey with both left and right hands.

But I use a two-handed rod because of the comfort, it's less fatiguing, I can control the fly better, I like holding onto the rod when I'm playing the fish. I can land them faster and I enjoy it. Not that I won't still fish a single-handed rod, but that is actually more wearing on me to do that.

Technique and Pattern
First of all I think there's probably one out of a thousand steelheaders that will catch a steelhead on a fly and only one out of a thousand of those fishermen will take one on a dead drift with a dry fly. This was a passion I had for about three years. I worked hard at it. I'm talking about an upstream cast or a downstream cast with lots of mending. It's not a grease-line technique.

Typically now, I'm going to say the last ten years, I take 1-2 fish a season with that method. It's not easy to do, it really isn't. The first time it happened it scared me to death. I went out and tried this, I cast the fly upstream and got a fish up, I saw him come up. I walked upstream about 30 feet so I could get a better angle for a dead drift and laid the fly over in the same spot and a fish came up and bumped the fly out of the water with its head.

I looked, and thought, did I really see that? I didn't hook that fish but I saw him. In that same season, this is back in '88 or '86 maybe, I was using a single-handed rod with a Royal Wulff.

I had three flies I used at that time: I used a Gray Wulff, Royal Wulff and a forest green steelhead Humpy. I like sizes 12-6.

I was obsessed with catching steelhead on a dry with a dead drift. It got so that I would give up a hundred fish to catch one on a dry fly on a dead drift. I think it was partly because I started reading Lee Wulff stories of Atlantic salmon fishing and I was just mesmerized.

I said, I know I can do it. Bill Alspach often said that he could catch a steelhead on a bare hook. Three times we went out with a hook and a fly called a Toy. It's basically a black hook with red thread or whatever color thread you want. Bill used red thread. He put a half hitch in it and landed a fish on the Snake River. He riffle hitched basically a bare hook.

The other one we did was a hook with silver tinsel and we caught fish with it using a riffle hitch. I had been riffle hitching since I started reading Lee Wulff in the 1970s. We liked to riffle hitch when nothing else was working. I don't think you really need to but sometimes it stirs a fish up.

I've got one technique I use for distance. You need to make about a 100 foot cast and it's basically an overhand cast with a two-handed rod or a good wind at your back Spey cast. After you get it out there, you just feed line and you're sliding the fly instead of swinging it with tension. You're actually sliding the fly down and all of a sudden a mouth will come up.

I only try the method when I think the conditions are just right. I'd say the best time is when that first run of fish comes in, when they are aggressive, hot and the water is down. If the water is up and running fast you don't have a chance, it swings too fast.

Two years ago, when we had low water, it was just ideal. There were some times when I had some fish boil on a wet fly and I switched to a dry fly and caught the fish. It's not the same as hunting for it using that technique. I still use my same three dry flies and a Muddler too.

The fly has got to be out in the river. I don't care what the pattern is. You gotta spend time in the river. When I talk to new people, I typically will notice a newbie by the number of false casts they make. One, two, three, four and they let it go to get another 3 feet of distance. That's a waste. You gotta spend more time with that fly in the water and not in the air. When I first started I tried many different patterns, often changing every 15 minutes, twenty in a day. Now, I don't think it matters that much what you have on, just have confidence in it and keep it in the water.

I've read all the books that talk about pattern. Pattern to me is more aesthetics. It's what I like to fish with, which is something pretty. I like the beauty and simplicity of an elegant fly. I will not fish an ugly fly. These guys with these Chernobyl Ants and stuff, isn't for me, sorry.

I like effective patterns that kind of have a range. I use about six different flies which include the Beats Me, Undertaker, Skunks, Dean River Green Lantern, and the Fall Favorite. I really like using traditional materials. I like using seal, polar bear, squirrel, golden pheasant crests I love. I like flies that I have developed called Pseudo Speys. Pseudo Spey meaning that they aren't tied with heron, they are tied with blue-eared pheasant or regular pheasant. I make short, low-profile patterns, very sparse.

My favorite steelhead fishing scenario is what I refer to as being a player at the table. I compare it to cards. When I get a steelhead up, all right, we're at the table! When I first started fishing I would go, did you see that? I missed it! Darn, oh gosh, and I would be upset because I lost my chance. Now I just salivate for the opportunity, cause we have a player. A player is a fish that's active that will come back. If I have a fish come up, I have a set established rhythm that I use.

I'll make the same exact cast again. No rest. I do the same exact thing again. I stop, regain my composure because it makes you hyperventilate. Make another cast. If he doesn't come up then I make two more casts upstream from it and two more casts downstream from it, and then I change flies. So I've made six casts, had him up on the first one and made five more.

Then I change flies and do exactly the same thing. Put two right where it was, two above it and two below it. I mean about 3 or 4 feet. If I don't get them up with that second fly I'll change to something totally different, a different color or size. I usually use a hook of the same size but I will change colors. If I'm using a Purple Green Butt I'll switch to a Beats Me or vice versa. If I switch to a third fly, many times I'll use a Muddler or a big Night Dancer or Disco Mouse, something totally different. After the third or fourth fly, if I haven't seen him again and I know its not early in the season when they're running through, I'll go about 20 feet upstream and come back on top of them with the first fly I raised them on.

If the fish is consistently coming at the flies, I had one come up to five different flies, I will go back to the first pattern and fish hard. Nine times out of ten it will hit that fly again. I just live for that moment; the more the better. I don't even care if I lose the card game, I mean you're dealing and it gives me the most adrenaline. Finally when I hook it, hooking it is almost secondary. It's that game you're playing.

For me, it's the game. Not exactly like cat and mouse, but more like a card game. Do I have the cards to catch this fish? A lot of times the fish wins, they don't come back. I've had multiple things happen. I've had fish come up multiple times on the same swing and nail it.

My biggest fish on the Snake was 19 pounds and that fish came up three times on the same drift. Finally it hit the fly in shallow water just a little ways down below me. It was a beautiful 39-inch male. I've had a few fish scare me when I've used Bombers. I don't catch many fish on Bombers. In fact, all the fish I've landed on Bombers you could count on two hands, but I've raised a lot of fish with Bombers and Muddlers.

I like to fish big Muddlers in size twos. Big heads, big things and I don't riffle hitch them. I don't need to. Just the tension on the water with the fly and the V and the gurgling that it's making is enough.

I fish another pattern called the Deer Turd which is deer hair, just a big round fly. It's made with black deer hair and a collar. It gurgles in the water. I like to use Bombers in smooth water. They have a real nice smooth V that they make. I raise fish with that and typically I switch to a Purple Green Butt or Beats Me to nail the fish.

There's a definite game to it and that's what I live for. A couple of years ago I only had one or two days out of 60 some that I didn't catch fish. It was real consistent.

I don't fish every day all day long; I fish through the fall, September-October almost every night. I'll leave and fish the last two hours of the day on the lower river. Ninety percent of my fish come during that last two hours of the day.

I don't get up that early anymore. I used to. To tell you the truth, fly-fishing first light can be good, but typically you live for the gray days, cloudy overcast days. They are miserable, people are sleeping in cause it's miserable. I'm out there. I'll fish all day on a cloudy day. I've had some of my best days in those conditions.

When the water gets much below 40 I may use a sink-tip line and a larger fly. When I'm fishing with someone and the water is 42 degrees, if they are fishing first through, they will have the floating line. I'll follow with a sink-tip. When the water gets down to 36-38 and you're pushing ice through the guides and the air temperature is 10, I'll fish a sink-tip. I'll use a bigger unweighted hook. I detest weighted flies.

I don't care to cast them. I make my own tapered leaders. I usually use 8-pound test most of the year until the big B's start to show up. I'll use 12-pound test then. I have landed my biggest fish in late September, I'm talking fish that are over 40 inches, over 20 pounds and some over 25, you want a little more than 8-pound test.

I've hooked fish in the tail before and I've had fish pop flies out of the water. I think out of every fish that you hook you have probably drawn the interest of 3-5 other fish. You never see them. To increase your odds in fishing you try to do some different things to put the cards in your hand, to play the best hand you can.

I really think when they are going for it and are curious and moving, something will make them decide yes or no and sometimes they may miss it. I don't know. I've hooked fish inside the mouth cavity. Normally I can tell how they are hooked just by the way they take. I don't set my hook. I drop my rod and let them pull, pull, pull. Then I may drop the rod to the side. I never set. Some people do, but I don't.

What I do is when I fish I keep a higher line than most people. Most people are fishing low. I don't fish that way. I fish it up, not straight up but I fish it up at least 45 degrees. I just hold it there. The minute I see that boil I drop that rod. When you drop a 15-foot rod you've got about 7 feet of slack, a lot of slack. Then I just wait. The tension will pull, pull, pull and then all I will do with that rod is to lay it over to the side toward the river bank. That way I feel the fly has had enough time for the fish to take it, put it in its mouth and turn on it and then they turn out normally. Those fish I typically hook in the left side of its mouth.

I don't worry about the fish spitting the hook out. When it's cold I've had fish pick up a fly and I've counted up to six, now that doesn't sound like much but with a sink-tip all of a sudden you'll feel tension, 1001, 1002, 1003, 1004, 1005, 1006 and then I tighten it up, even then I won't do a hard set. Just sit there, now a lot of times the fly will come out but I've had them come back. Normally when they feel the hook they get pretty gun shy. That's my way of doing it. It works for me.

I've caught 8 fish over 20 pounds and I have caught one that measured 44 1/2 inches which I will tell you about. I went out and was using a pattern called a Purple Bash with a riffle hitch with 10 pound test and my 13 1/2 foot Sage. I got a fish up. I cast again and I hooked him. But this fish didn't budge. Within that first ten minutes I finally edged him over close to me and I'm kind of on a steep bank and had no place to land him.

I'm thinking that it might be a large salmon he was so huge. He never jumped, he acted like he didn't know he was hooked. I muscled him over literally, and when he saw me he took off like a bat out of hell out into the river and then downstream and then he jumped twice. Big fish. The reel is just singing. I was using a Loop Reel with 120 yards of line plus the fly line, on that light 13 foot rod. I played that fish for 55 minutes.

I finally got down as far as I could wade and got to the point where I had to make a stand. I knew if I could work him into the slack water I had a chance, but if he went down the middle of the river he would be gone. It went into the slack water. When I landed that fish and got him in, my knees were shaking, my eyes were glazed and I was just drained and dumbfounded. I did have enough sense to measure it and I revived it. It was a hatchery fish. My dad's fish, which was almost 45 inches in 1985, was a hatchery fish also.

One time I caught two twenties in one day, which was a real thrill. I think I might have hooked a third, it was scary. It was early in September and hooked this big beautiful fish and fought him quite a while, 40 minutes, landed him, it was 42 inches. I went up river a ways, hooked another fish and it just dogged me. Big fish kind of throb the rod, they don't, they will make some nice big runs, but they give a deep throb and you know that they are just huge.

It finally got off, I lost it. I fished through the run again and landed a fish that was 40 inches. It had big, thick shoulders, and this one only took me 15 minutes to land. The first fish I caught on a Muddler, the second one was on a Dean River Lantern 2/0. Sometimes when the big fish come in even in early fall I may use a large hook. Even if the water is low and clear I will switch to a big fly at times. Not that they won't take a small fly because the biggest fish I landed was on a number 4 Purple Bash which is kinda like a Purple Peril, but a little different.

If you are out on the river and see fish rolling I have found that sometimes it is really hard to get them to come back and be a player. You might catch one moving, but I catch more on cloudy, drizzly days that have taken people off the river and during a weekday.

Bill Alspach

Bill Alspach (right) and ex-Governor Cecil Andrus (left) on Kelly Creek in northern Idaho. Bill was the originator of the "Beats Me" steelhead fly which is a popular local pattern.

When I was conducting interviews for this book, the name Bill Alspach came up quite a bit and people who knew him said that it would be very appropriate to include Bill's contributions to steelheading in the area. Most of the information provided below comes from his best friend Craig Lannigan and his wife Angie.

Background

Bill was born in Lewiston in 1942 and was introduced to the Clearwater and other rivers by his dad who he fished with a lot. He started fly-fishing in the early 1970s shortly after he had experienced his first heart attack. Angie says he wanted to do something that was a little more relaxing and he spent many hours practicing how to cast on their front lawn. He was determined to be a good caster and by all accounts Bill could cast a fly better than most.

Angie and Bill grew up together and were neighbors in north Lewiston from the age of four. They were married for 32 years. After his first heart attack the doctor told Bill that he should live life to the fullest and that is one of the reasons why he spent a lot of time on the local rivers that he dearly loved.

Craig Lannigan said, "Back when I first started, there just weren't very many fly-fishermen period. Then I ran into Bill Alspach who had lived here all his life. He had great stories about steelheading up on the North Fork of the Clearwater. Bill fished all his life on the local rivers, but didn't start serious fly-fishing till after his first heart attack in the early 70s.

Bill was one of the few that fished for steelhead with his dad on the North Fork before Dworshak. He was probably one of the few. He had stories about the 25-pound fish up there that

The Beats Me is a popular local steelhead pattern that is credited to the late Bill Alspach.

Beats Me
(tied by Dave Clark)

Hook: Partridge Wilson or Tiemco 79089 sizes 8-4
Thread: Black
Body: Back half: pink nylon tying thread; Front half: black chenille
Rib: #18 silver mylar (tied just over the pink)
Hackle: Webby grizzly (three turns tied over the chenille)
Wing: Squirrel tail or white calf tail

would oftentimes spool you. There was no way to stop them. He was pretty much self-taught. Just watching his technique, it was completely different than anyone I've seen, even to this day. His casting was perfect. I don't know where he learned how to do it. He read a lot of books. He was a good double-hauler. He could really shoot a fly line.

I watched LeRoy Hyatt's fly-tying show the other day and he was tying a Beats Me. That was Bill's famed steelhead fly. Probably one of the best steelhead flies in this area. The first one Bill gave me; I landed thirteen steelhead on the Grande Ronde, after watching him land three in one hour. I said, "What is it you're using," and he said, "Beats me!" That was his original fly. He actually told me that he tried to model it from an emerging caddis. It does have a large thorax and it has qualities of that, and he actually tried to imitate that with that design, although it turned into a bright-colored fly.

Bill Alspach died of a heart attack on February 12, 1997. I fished with him on February 9 on the Grande Ronde. We were going to meet up at the fly-caster's meeting in Pullman on Monday in the evening and he passed away at noon while swimming in the pool.

Bill Alspach Steelhead Story by Craig Lannigan
I had a meeting after school in the evening a while back. The meeting was at 9:00. It was in the fall when it still didn't get dark till around 9:00. I had to be in, but I had about 1 1/2 hours to fish. Bill Alspach was fishing the lower river and I could see him, so I yelled at him and asked him how he was doing. He said, "Great! I haven't caught any fish yet." Just at that moment the fly swung across and this fish came up, stopped, paused, quivered, boiled at the fly and went back down. I'm watching all this.

"Did you see that," I yelled. Bill, said, "Yep, I saw it." I'm going, what fly do you have on? It was a Beats Me. On the second cast, the fish did the same exact thing, it came out of nowhere, paused, quivered its fins, moved to the fly, boiled and then went back down.

You get a lump in your heart when this is going on. So Bill cast again and the fish did the exact same thing, came up, quivered, opened it's mouth, sipped the fly and zoomed off down the river. Three times it did exactly the same thing, but the third time it took the fly. I'm watching this the whole time. So you know, he's playing this fish and its headed out toward this boat. I'm going, I know he's going to land it, so I run back to my rig to get my waders and rod. I didn't land a fish that night and I was late for the meeting. He landed it; it was a 12 pound hen, mint-silver fish. I learned a lot from watching that fish come up quivering there like it was debating what to do.

LeRoy Hyatt

Local celebrity and expert fly tier Leroy Hyatt with a Clearwater steelhead in 1999.

LeRoy Hyatt has lived in the Lewiston Valley since 1972 and has established an outstanding reputation as a professional fly tier. He absolutely loves to tie flies and he especially loves to tie some of the more challenging patterns like Muddler Minnows, Bombers, Goddard Caddises, Madame X and others that involve spinning and trimming deer and elk hair. LeRoy is active in the community and works with youth groups and junior high students in fly-tying clinics.

LeRoy teamed with the late Dave Engerbretson a well-known fly-fisherman from Moscow, Idaho a few years ago to produce a successful television show on fly tying. They have produced a video of that series and new shows are being produced for next year. LeRoy also works part time at the Traditional Sportsman fly shop in Lewiston where he can be observed tying flies and dispensing advice.

Leroy: There was a guy I worked with in Idaho Falls that invited me over to his house one time and I watched him tie some flies on his kitchen table. I was totally enthralled. I came back home, ordered a vise and some hooks and stuff from Herters. I knew no one that tied flies. I taught myself. If there was anything that could be done wrong, I did it. I kept practicing, practicing on anybody I could find at a show to help me out. I started progressing and got a little better.

We then moved to Lewiston in the early 70s. Again, I was still trying to tie flies. The guys I worked with kept talking about steelhead. Steelhead, I knew nothing of what a steelhead was other than just a big rainbow trout. I found a pattern, the old Skunk, I had an old 7 1/2 foot pack rod. I didn't know any better. The reel I had thank goodness would hold enough line and backing, it was an old Pflueger model 1495, I can still remember it. I had a pair of chest waders, no felt soles just rubber boots and I thought this was going to be okay, I'm going to go do it.

I'll never forget across from the old rodeo grounds out here I hooked my first steelhead. I ran a lot, I fell down a lot, I chased that fish up and down the river. I didn't get it in, I can still see to this day that fish standing on its head out there in about two feet of water with his tail out of the water. He's rubbing his nose on the bottom; I know what he is doing.

I'm using a two-hander. I started off, oh man, 15 years ago with a 13 1/2 foot 7 weight. In fact, Craig Lannigan and I were probably the first to have double-handed rods here. Jim Green built me a shooting head and that's what I learned with. I caught a lot of fish on that rod. The Spey casting just totally enthralled me. I went to a double-taper line thinking that would be the way to go. I fought that rod. Finally, I knew a guy that worked for Rio and he got me into one of their wind cutters and that solved most of my problems. Since then I've gone to a 15 foot rod, it is much easier to cast, much much easier.

The guys I fish with, we use a floating line and probably until the water temperature gets down into the real low 40s and maybe one of us will go to a sink-tip. The other one will stay with a floating line. Always a long leader though and see which one starts picking up fish and then we will switch whichever way we need to go.

I've caught fish in the 18-19 pound range with my 7-weight 13 1/2 foot two-handed rod and I love the feel of those fish. I don't lose as many fish with that two-handed rod because of the give of that rod. I just don't lose as many.

I will not overhand cast with my rod. I made myself learn the right- and left-hand casts. Most of the time I fish on the left bank so I'm using a double-hand left or a single Spey. You know Jimmy Green helped me with this, he told me, "If you're going to buy a two-handed rod just to get the distance, save your money." He said, "What you're looking for is the line control." And he's right, he's very right. I really feel that with a two-handed rod I can keep my fly in the water at least 30% longer than a guy with a single-handed rod because all I've gotta do is strip in 6-8 strips of line and with a simple movement I'm right back in the water again.

I've heard that a lot of the guys are fishing steelhead with dropper flies, but I've not tried that. They are using two wet flies, a large one and a small one at the same time. When I use a dropper for trout I don't tie the upper fly on the leader, I just slide it up the leader and then tie the knot and then tie your dropper on. The dropper fly is just going to slide up and down that leader. If you hook a fish with that upper fly the knot will never pull through the eye and you can land the fish.

I don't even carry a fly box, when I'm steelhead fishing I don't even wear a vest. Most of my fly patterns you will never find in a book. I just dream up a lot of my steelhead flies. I think that with steelhead patterns, black is often overlooked for surface and subsurface flies, especially on a dark or overcast day or evening because that fish is looking up into a sky a whole lot lighter than what you are seeing looking down into that black water.

I've really become excited about Spey flies. I don't tie them traditionally; I don't go out and buy that Spey hackle and all that expensive stuff. I use a lot of marabou. Marabou is probably the cheapest Spey hackle you will get. It won't last as long as some of the other stuff, but it still gives the same action. I'm also playing a lot more with products from Anglers Sport Group out of New York. They sell a material called Bowtier, which is an arctic

Bombers
(tied by LeRoy Hyatt)
Body: Deer hair with palmered black hackle
Tail: Black elk or moose hair

*Clipped deer-hair patterns like
Bombers are some of LeRoy's favorites.*

fox, and they also have something that comes from Finnish raccoon that they dye in multiple colors. That Finnish raccoon will fit over a 2/0 hook and it will totally encompass that whole hook and go about an inch beyond and it gives the same action as marabou but it's much more durable, so I've been playing with that a lot.

The traditional patterns that you see in books, I don't fish much with them. I really firmly believe that it doesn't really matter what you have on the end of your leader, it's if you get one in front of his face that agitates him enough he is going to move it aside, regardless of pattern. Sometimes I will use a Fall Favorite or Skunk, but mostly just my own stuff. I am firmly of the opinion that for the last several years the majority of my flies have been black, purple or orange. I don't go for all those other colors.

I know when I was fishing with Trey Combs that he loves a big Bomber. In fact I still tie Bombers for Trey. He uses Bombers on a new river just as a searching pattern. He will go really quick. He will skate that fly through, if he finds a player that doesn't take, he will go back with a small wet fly and will normally pick the fish up. He says, that way I can cover water real fast.

I use surface patterns sometimes, but not as much as I used to. I've caught quite a few on surface flies. If you have cholesterol problem, I guarantee it will greatly reduce your cholesterol to see that great big hummer come up there; it looks like somebody turned a great big wash tub upside down. I find that I consistently catch more fish by using a large-hackled fly, such as a Spey fly. I use a lot of 1/0 and 2/0 hooks. I will occasionally use a size 6 but not very often. If I'm going dry-fly, always 6's and 8's.

I skate Muddlers sometimes, but I don't use a riffle hitch. I can tie enough knots on my own without tying one on purpose.

You know I may not catch as many fish as some guys that riffle them, but hey I've caught my share and I'm having fun and that's what counts. Sometimes I will use a small black Muddler in a size 10 or 8.

In the winter I use flies with the longest webbiest hackle that I have and I will always put a wrap or two of that and then some kind of a duck feather or something in front of that marabou, plus as you are casting sometimes that marabou has a tendency to crawl over the top of your leader. That feather in front of that hackle will keep that marabou from doing that. I don't like the true Popsicle-type pattern, once you pick it up to cast it you pump water out of it, it takes too long for that fly, to get back down to fishing right again unless you are using a sinking line or weighted fly but I normally don't like to weight my flies. A big factor in choosing a fly is if you have confidence in it.

I use 12-foot leaders and 8-pound test. Sometimes I will go to a 10 if I go to a sink-tip with only a 4-5 foot leader. Do you know what, I have fished with an awful lot of leaders over the years and I will invariably come back to that Maxima leader. I tie my own. I start with a 6-foot section of 25 pound test and sometimes 30, then I go 3 feet, 1.5 feet and then the tippet. It's a formula I saw in a magazine from Lefty Kreh. I know some guys use 40- and 50-pound butt sections, I don't like it that heavy because it can overload your fly line and they will start clicking that fly line, it's too heavy. That 25-pound butt section is just wonderful, even on my trout fishing I will start off with a 20-pound section and go down to a 12-foot leader.

I'm not a big fan of using a strike indicator myself. I tend to agree that it is not true fly-fishing and is not much of an art. Sometimes I will put a bead eye on a fly but not very often.

Usually just a good sink-tip line will get you as deep as you need. I was speaking at a banquet one time and I made the statement that fly-fishing is a lot easier than people give it credit for.

Stories

I remember rather vividly one time I got all my honey do's done and I headed up the Clearwater to a favorite run On the fifth cast I hung a beautiful fish that just hammered me. It jumped five times and on the fifth jump landed in the rock on the bank. So I hurried and ran down there and the hook had fallen out. I got there and got her, by the tail, it was a wild fish about 15 pounds. It took me a long time to revive her but I held her in the water for a long time. That was a fun trip; I was all by myself, not another soul there to see it. I'll always remember that one.

I really think you remember the fish you lose as much as the ones you'll catch. I wake up at night thinking, Man, what did I do wrong, what could I do differently. We were fishing two years ago on the Clearwater and I put a fly on and I was the first one in the hole For some reason my line was tangled on my reel and I was standing there untangling that backlash when, bang, a steelhead hit and it came out of the water and it was a big fish and it immediately ran away from me and I can still feel that rod as it came to the end of that backlash and the hook pulled loose and the fish came unbuttoned. I thought he broke me off, I brought the fly back in and the hook was totally straightened.

Needless to say, now I'm very careful how I wind my line on the reel because I can remember that fish and remember him coming up out of the water the sun down below me, and I could see that spray coming off him; yeah, every steelhead you catch is a memorable experience.

I've always told people that I'd rather go with a guy and watch him catch his first steelhead on a fly than catch one myself. You'll bloody your knuckles on that reel trying to stop that reel from spinning and you will be so excited that you will back up 30 feet out of the water trying to drag that fish to shore. Your eyes are twice as big around. No, I love it, you just sit there and laugh and watch those people, I have a good time.

Steelhead fishing is a lot of casting, a lot of casting and if you are not doing any good pretty soon you get tired and your casting goes to pot. Some of my most memorable days I have never caught a fish. I'm not in it for the numbers anymore; I've caught enough fish that I don't need that. One fish is a good day. Last year on the Ronde, we were down there for three days, on the first day the two of us hooked 11 fish and it was a good day.

One day after work I ran up the Clearwater and hooked three and landed two in one hour, which to me is unbelievable. I know the Steve Pettits and Keith Stonebrakers can catch fish in a toilet. They know exactly where to go and what to do and how to do it. To me it's still a whole lot of chuck and chance it. I don't care what anyone tells you. The skill is getting the presentation out there and hoping you get a good swing on the fly. That doesn't always happen; you can't always put that fly where you want it. I can't, maybe some can. No, one fish I am as happy as I can be, two fish maybe a little happier. I don't know. I've had some really good times just out on the river fishing without touching a fish and just watching wildlife and birds. We have driven down on the Ronde and watched deer and sheep and didn't even fish, ate lunch and came home and tied flies and we had a good time.

1980s

Gordie Olsen

Gordie Olsen with a Grande Ronde steelhead.

Gordie Olsen is an engineer who works in Spokane and spends his leisure time fly-fishing. Gordie has been fishing with Jake Gulke on the Grande Ronde since 1980 and has collaborated with Jimmy Green on building and designing Spey rods and lines. He fly-fishes for steelhead on the Kispiox in British Columbia on a regular basis and some of his flies have been included in fly-tying books.

Gordie: When I was little growing up in Chewaleh, WA, I caught my first fish at age six in Chewelah Creek in the park. My neighbor was an elderly gentleman that got me into fishing with a fly. From that day on I always thought it was a cool way to fish. Later, when I got into high school, I started tying my own flies and doing a lot of fly-fishing on my own in places like Sheep Creek and Mill Creek and the lakes around there.

When I went on to college at Bozeman, Montana in 1964, there was a lot of pristine rivers and very few fishermen. I got to fish a lot of the spring creeks and the Jefferson, Madison, and Yellowstone. I met Jake Gulke in Colville in the late 70s. He was working for Washington Water Power and we got together and formed a fly club up there, with 4, or 5 other people, called the Upper Columbia Flyfisher's. Jake had always been into fly-fishing for steelhead in the fall, whereas, I had always spent my falls

in Montana or Colorado hunting elk or deer. He finally convinced me to come down to the Grande Ronde in 1980 and try fly-fishing.

I was hunting in Idaho at the time and happened to get an elk the first or second day so I had a lot of time left. I swung by the Grande Ronde on the way home and attempted for several days to catch a fish on a fly. Jake was catching them all the time. I didn't have any flies, I was using his flies. It took a little art to it and finally on the fifth or sixth day I landed my first one. I had hooked some before that, but never got them in, they always got the best of me.

I landed that first fish on the lower Ronde and really from that day on I gave up hunting and concentrated on fly-fishing for steelhead. Now we start fly-fishing in the spring for trout and fish right on through to December for steelhead.

I caught my first fish on a Green Butt Skunk. Not knowing anything about steelhead flies, I went to some books and tied some Purple Perils, Skykomish Sunrises, and Skunks. I fished those for several years before we started experimenting and gained a little more confidence in trying other things.

Jake was experimenting with a lot of flashy materials and I started using a lot of marabou because I like the undulation of the marabou in the current. Also being soft, I figured in the cold still water that the fish may hang onto it longer. They are a lot easier to tie, you don't have to worry about French tinsels, expensive type hackles and what not. So the past few years I've experimented with different color combinations of marabou. I'm also using arctic fox; it gives the fly a little more silhouette and bulks up a little bigger.

I came up with a purple and cerise fly, it's a marabou fly, I now use it about 80% of the time on either a dry or sink-tip line. It doesn't seem to make any difference. I used to tie a lot of different sizes, I used to use a lot of 4's and 6's on the Ronde, but I found out once I went up to Canada that those fish would straighten those hooks out, so I started tying 2/0's up there and I said, you know, why have all these other sizes, I'll use a 2/0 down on the Ronde.

I catch a lot of fish with them. I was always told back in my days as a lake fisherman that if you wanted to catch big fish you need to use a big fly, so I use a big fly. If I get a pull I will switch patterns. If no one is in the run with me, I will let the fish rest a little and then go back with the same pattern. If someone is behind me, I will put something different on and try again. Sometimes that works.

I do know that fish will take pretty rapidly. One Friday night I got off work and drove 90 mph to get down to the Ronde. Jake

Purple and Charise Marabou Fly
(tied by Gordie Olsen)
Body: Purple and charise marabou with some crystal flash

This fluffy marabou fly is original with Gordie Olsen.

was already in our favorite run, so I got in behind him and after about 15 minutes I had a fish. As I was landing it, Jake told me to take a look at it and see if it had a small hunk out of the side of its mouth. I landed it and looked at it and sure enough a small piece was missing from the side of its mouth. Jake said, "I caught that fish 20 minutes ago."

That was a fish that was pretty stupid. I do believe that for some reason those fish are just simply reacting. With steelhead it seems like the gaudier the fly the better. I think a lot of people tie steelhead flies really to impress other steelhead fishermen. I don't think it makes much difference to the fish. For the most part, I don't think color makes a lot of difference. I think there are some colors that show up better in turbid waters and that's where I think the advantage is.

I think in gin-clear water where the fish can see, the color doesn't make a difference. The fish is going to see it. When you get in your dark waters, I think purples and blacks are going to silhouette up better.

I know on the Dean we had a glacial till river one year. Jake always liked to use orange, 'cause orange is a very popular steelhead color and I was stuck with my purple. I said, let's just have a little test, so we waded out in a dead spot where the water was 3-4 feet deep and we dropped the flies in the water. The orange fly was invisible to the human eye after one foot.

I dropped that purple one down there and we could see it all the way down to 2 1/2 feet. You could see the darkness of it. Bass fishermen know this too. They have that fancy color locator that they put down there and select a color based on the turbidity and so on. I think color makes a difference in dirty water and makes no difference in clean water.

The biggest fish I caught on the Snake was 38 1/2 inches, it was a wild buck so it was a good fish. It was 18 or 19 poundss.

Jim Green and Spey Rods

I met Jimmy Green in 1982 when the conclave was held in Spokane. I got one of the first Fenwick graphite rods from Jimmy. I wanted to meet him. I watched him and Harry Lemire fish together down at the mouth of the Ronde.

I kept telling Jake that we ought to go up and introduce ourselves to Jimmy Green. We had heard through the grapevine that he had heard of us and wanted to meet us. Jake said, why do we want to go up and talk to him. He says, we know as much as he does and I says, no we don't. So I was driving back from fishing and I said, dammit, it's the middle of the day, the fish aren't biting, we're going to go up and introduce ourselves to Jimmy Green.

So we went up to Jimmy's house and introduced ourselves and gee whiz, he was more than glad to meet us and was happy that we went up there. We started talking fishing and it wasn't long before we realized that when it came to casting and rods that we didn't have a clue what was going on in the real world.

At that time Jake and I were strictly fishing one-handed rods. We had been fishing the Dean River in Canada for 4-5 years and we always used one-handed rods. But we noticed these guys with two-handed rods one time and they were just splashing the water and we said, 'my heck, why would anybody want to go to all that work to catch a fish.' It looked like they were in pain.

We said, that's not for us, but when we got up to Jimmy's we found out that Jimmy was exclusively a two-hander and held the world record in casting; and I do believe he was the first person to cast over 200 feet. He had a bunch of two-handed Sage rods there and he had us try them.

We tried casting out back on his lawn and we couldn't do very much. He told us to keep working on it. So from that day on we stopped in and he would practice with us and pretty soon we got pretty good. He gave us a couple of rods to use and told us to go out on the river and try them out.

Well, we would go up the river and get out of sight where no one could see us, because we couldn't cast very well. We'd hit ourselves in the back of the head or neck. There was all sorts of stuff that went wrong. Pretty soon we were casting about 75 feet and I didn't think life was going to get any better because the key to two-handed casting is to use your lower hand not your right hand, if you are a right-handed caster. It's the left hand that does all the work.

Once you've got the rhythm and learn how to stop the rod then you started seeing more distance and more control. Soon we were casting pretty good and we said 'hey, let's build us a two-handed rod.' We got some blanks from Jimmy and built some and started fishing with them, but we couldn't find a decent line.

We started making our own lines because we figured according to Jimmy that the weights on these rods meant nothing. Some of these rods were way underloaded. In order to come up with something different we wanted to generate a lot of weight in a short distance. Jimmy was a strict believer in the overhand cast. He thought Spey casting was for sissies.

Lately I see a lot of new people fishing different methods. One of the most lethal methods is using a weighted fly and a bobber. It's just bobber-and-jig fishing on a fly rod, it's the same thing. On the Grande Ronde this method is lethal. People are yarding them out and they aren't moving much either. I saw people this year take 20 fish doing that.

It's kind of sad. It's a legal method, but there's no skill involved. You don't cast or mend. You figure out how deep the water is and set your bobber a little less than that deep. I've not brought myself to use that method, but to each his own.

I do cast surface flies, it's a lot of fun with a floating line. We don't fish dry flies if the temperature is below 48-50 degrees. You're probably going to catch more fish if you're down. The colder the water gets, the less active the fish become. I like Bomber type patterns, a Waller Waker, and spun deer-hair flies.

If no one else is around I won't wade out. I fish as close to the shore as possible. I've been know to wade too deep. I've been swept down the Snake three times when I thought I was a goner for getting careless. In the Grande Ronde you don't have to throw a lot of line. A one-handed rod is more than ample in most places. I try to cover as much water as possible. We will fish to dark and in the full moon.

When we were younger we used to get up at 4:00 in the morning and get in the run at dark to be the first ones through. There's some advantage to being the first one in line. You get first crack if they are there. As you get older, it really isn't that important, we used to think we had to catch every fish in the river, but not anymore. I've caught quite a few fish in the 34-inch class that were pretty impressive. I haven't caught any 20-pounders on the Ronde like I have in Canada.

One time I hooked a fish on the Ronde, Jake was fishing below me. I wasn't sure how big this fish was because the big ones always get away. But it acted like some of the wild fish in Canada. Once he took the hook he headed straight out for the Snake and I was spooled before I could do anything. I never had a chance. He didn't belong there and he knew it. That was the hottest fish I ever hooked. He jumped a lot and was out of the water when he went by Jake.

I learned early on that steelhead etiquette has rules just like golf. You just don't go out and get in a run. You go to the back of the run and take your turn. You cast and you move six feet downstream and don't hog one spot. Early on there was no problem with this. In the evening we would fish the Social Security Run and there would be 6-7 of us going round like a big wheel. We would catch 10-12 fish in an evening. Through the years there are more people down there using gear which is fine with me but some of these people never move.

Now you don't see many fly-fishermen down in front. There are places now where the fly-fishermen just won't go. I was down there this year and I saw 20-30 people and none of them will move. If one doesn't move, then none of them move.

They are casting for moving fish, whereas a fly-fisherman moves through a run and when he catches fish he remembers the place. There's either a rock down there or a dish-tub hole, a washout, for some reason it's a resting fish. Some waters you know when you're getting close, so you get prepared because you know your chances are good of getting a take. That gives everybody a fair shot; you cover water, go to the back and go through again. Everybody has the same chance to fish the same water, there was never any complaints.

Now there's people who haven't heard of this who come down and know how to cherry pick and so now they jump in and keep it all to themselves. I remember about eight years ago there were three gentlemen from Spokane. Never been steelheading before. They got down in a run in the morning and they commenced to catch fish after fish and they didn't move.

Myself and Moe Clucking were there. They were catching fish so they were reluctant to move. So a couple of my friends asked them if they would mind moving so the rest of us could have a chance to fish. They said, 'no, we're not moving.' They were fly-fishing, first time out.

Before the day was over, we were told that they landed 32 fish and lost a lot more. At 5:00 I was party to a group that was threatening them with physical harm if they didn't get their butts out of the water. That's the closest thing I've seen to a fight down there. When we tried to tell them what the rules were they didn't care. There should be a book about it, like golf does.

That night we were sitting around the fire saying someone has got to teach these guys. So the next morning we decided to get in their first. As I was driving up there the next morning I could see flashlights out there. It looked like about 11 people were in there. The word was out. I said, 'Well, there is no use of me getting in there,' so I went up above. There was nobody there, I started fishing at daybreak and when the sun came up I was the only one in the run and on my first pass through there I landed nine fish. I happened to be in the right place at the right time and that's what steelhead fishing is to me.

The people down below me were hooking lines and swearing at each other 'cause it had been such a great place the day before. Just because one place is good one day doesn't mean that those fish will still be there. They could be miles up the river.

Mac Huff

Mac Huff of Joseph, with a Grande Ronde steelhead taken with a Red Bunny Leech.

JIM HEPWORTH

Mac Huff lives in Joseph, Oregon and has been a professional fishing guide for fifteen years. He manages Eagle Cap Guide Service and provides fishing and natural history excursions on the Grande Ronde and other local rivers. He has as much experience fly-fishing the Grande Ronde as anyone I know, and most of his clientele are steelhead fly-fishermen. He has probably caught as many steelhead on a fly as any other of the local fly-fishers.

Mac: I grew up in central Oregon around Sisters, hunted and fished all my life. I have never outgrown it. I have been fly-fishing since I was nine. My dad taught me. I was fortunate. My dad was a game warden who fished and hunted. He was always outdoor oriented. He loved to fly-fish. He passed that heritage on to me and it truly is a heritage. It was something that was pretty important to him and he passed that on to me.

I eventually got a degree in wildlife biology from Oregon State and got a job with the Oregon Department of Fish and Wildlife doing surveys for them near Enterprise, Oregon in

1976. At the end of the summer I was to broke too leave so I've been over here ever since.

I eventually ended up owning a sporting goods store which really was a fly shop in summer and a ski shop in winter. With that came an opportunity to start guiding and I've been doing that ever since. I own my own guide service called Eagle Cap Fishing Guides. I started guiding out of Bogan's in 1988 and after a few years I was developing enough clients of my own to go buy my own boat. So in 1994 I developed a strong interest in starting my own business. Before I started guiding I had been fly-fishing for steelhead on the Ronde for 8-10 years before that, so I have about 23 years here on the river.

Guides and Outfitter System

Oregon and Washington have different systems when it comes to guiding on the rivers. Basically in Washington you just have to show up. Anyone can be a guide. The State is more than willing to cash a check and you're a guide. Anyone can get a guide's license, you don't even need to be a resident. Washington has not sanctified the Wild and Scenic Regulation on the river here.

Oregon did sanctify the Wild and Scenic Regulation so there you have to have a permit. Not only do you have to have a guide's license, but you have to have a Federal Use Permit. There are thirty of them that are allowed. They were given out on a first-come, first-served basis and I was definitely one of the last. If you want to get in the business today, you would have to buy out one of the outfitters.

An outfitter is not limited to the number of boats they can put on the water each day. They can put out as many as they want. One of the local outfitters last year put out 20 pontoon boats. I wish Washington would do like Idaho and limit the number of boats an outfitter can put out each day. It's an ugly situation.

I kind of taught myself how to fly-fish for steelhead. I can remember my first steelhead on a fly. It was actually the first day that I had ever gone steelheading with a fly rod. I had an 8-weight Lamiglas rod. I had purchased a rod with steelhead in mind, that was my focus.

Not knowing any better, I was dead-drifting a Silver Hilton and had actually had a fish on 20 minutes before. It really surprised me. I then moved up into water that I don't fish much anymore, but it was in some white water and I pulled this fish out of a pocket on an upstream cast, dead-drifting.

The line stopped and it wouldn't come loose. I had watched "Fishing the West" and they had talked about Silver Hiltons on that show so I tied up some. I've actually been quite successful with that pattern over the years.

So then over the next six years I spent a lot of time learning. I was catching about a dozen fish a year. Basically, when I would

Mac Huff fishes several colors of the Bunny Leech during the winter on the Grande Ronde.

Bunny Leech
(tied by Dan Landeen)

Body: Rabbit fur strip

finally get one and actually land it, I would sit there when it was over and say, 'okay, what happened? What was different this time?'

So in serving my apprenticeship, the breakthrough to go from a dozen fish a year to 100-200 a year was developing a feel to know when a fish took. At that point then I could go back and catch the fish say on the second or third cast quite often, or simply recognize the take, that soft pull when he took it and set the hook instead of waiting for him to hook himself.

The first bunch of years I caught most of my fish almost exclusively dead-drifting. It's not that hard to catch steelhead that way despite what you may have read or heard. I will occasionally use a strike indicator and that technique has allowed me to catch a lot more fish, because on a 20 foot cast it is really hard to tell if your line darts away.

So that's what would be happening. As I would work out further, you know the more water you can cover the more fish you're going to find. It would get out there and now I would know that I had a take. The indicator doesn't even have to sink, it can be under water; you just need to see it move underneath the water.

I don't spend much time anymore tying leaders or tying flies. That stuff cuts into my fishing time. There are bargains out there. There are people that are happy to sit in a little cubicle and tie those flies so I can spend more time on the river.

As far as patterns go, I tell people to use what works. I find that for myself I will get intrigued with a particular pattern, say a Silver Hilton, and I will try it and I will be damned if it doesn't work. Then maybe I will try a Freight Train and I will be damned, it works and then I will see something like a Surgeon General and I'll be damned, it works too.

Pretty soon I come to the conclusion that maybe the fly is not the most important thing. You have to use something that you're confident in. When you do that you find that the fly doesn't make any difference. There's days that I've had a fly definitely make the difference. But day in and day out the fly is secondary.

For clients I usually start them out with a dark fly. I will often start with a dark Woolly Bugger. I like the purples. The majority of the flies I use are on the dark side of the spectrum, but I've had days where I've done better with brighter colors. I also catch a lot of fish on patterns with a lot of orange in them, such as orange Woolly Buggers and Polar Shrimps.

I will fish surface patterns when I'm fishing for myself. I have trouble convincing clients to use surface patterns. That's one of those confidence things. Very often clients don't really believe that those patterns will work. They need to keep throwing it if it's going to work. There are lots of opportunities to do it if I had clients who wanted to do it.

They don't believe it. I've had cases where I've put a surface fly on and sent the guy out and within a dozen casts they've had fish come up and whack it. Then he was convinced. But I've also had cases where the fellow has had fish hit the fly basically on the surface and so I switched them over to flies that would fish on the surface and they make a couple of casts and say, 'Well, this isn't working right.'

And so then I have to change it back. They saw the fish hit at the top and still didn't believe what they saw. That's some of the things you learn as a guide. For me, I've learned there's lots of ways to catch fish and the person that's here is here for some recreation, as well as to catch fish, you know some enjoyment and some relaxation. We don't need to butt heads. We can go to a subsurface pattern or use a sink-tip if they want. We find a common ground.

I typically riffle hitch all of my surface flies. Just to help the fly stay on the surface. It makes a big difference. Some of the real thin patterns I will riffle hitch in the middle of the hook, just T bone that hook to make it come to the surface. You can riffle a bare hook, but you have to tie it way back so it will turn perpendicular to the current.

There's nothing like a steelhead coming up to take a fly on the surface. I can remember one run where I was using a waking fly. Since that was my purpose to take one on the top, you'd think I'd be ready, but all of a sudden my fly was standing on a hill of water about a foot above the normal level of the river.

That's all, it just rose up, it levitated. My eyes kinda got big, all of a sudden this nose sticks through with this big gaping mouth and the fly disappeared. I couldn't stand still and I jerked the fly right out of his mouth. The fish slowly rolled over and closed on air. I'm going nuts. They are so slow in the million heartbeats that happen from the time that their nose pokes through until they close, it's an eternity. What a memorable fish! Even at missing him.

If I've had a pull this is usually what I do. What happens on those for me is that you'll go through, you know, you cast and you move, you cast and you move. Then you feel that little kiss and you think, 'oh yeah.' You put the same cast back, not where the fish hit, you put the same cast back and usually when that fly comes through you'd better be hanging onto your rod because there ain't nothing subtle about that one.

Oh man, it's like fish which you may or may not know have an etiquette. Okay in other words, like anything else they've got a spot and they are going to maintain a space and when something comes into that space they are going to do things to move it out. Among the first things they do is probably something like eye contact, posturing, posturing definitely. But there are things that go on in nature that we are not quite up on yet.

Jeff Jarrett

It can be something as simple as eye contact. Well, this foreign object, your fly, doesn't see that so it goes on through, so the fish comes up and gives it a little encouragement to get out of there. Wel, a short time later, here comes that fly again. Well, you impertinent bastard, Bam! You are going to learn this time!

You know, that seems to be what happens. They do their posturing, that doesn't work, so then probably as much as anything they give it a nudge which is a minimum expenditure of energy on their part, just to get the message through to this thing that it's moving into their space. The next time the fly comes through, they've had it. I've had that happen to me a lot.

So then the other thing to do is to change patterns. One time I was guiding two people and I was helping a guy upstream. I came down and asked the other guy how he was doing and he said, "I had one hit out there."

"All right, let's see what happens." So he throws a few casts through and nothing happens. Okay, let's change flies. We changed to a Silver Hilton and the first drift through he gets a little pull. Try it again. A dozen drifts, nothing. Well, let's change again. We changed to a purple Woolly Bugger. We drifted it through and on the first cast that fish just munched it. So we got that fish. If you don't poke them too hard there's a good chance you can still get them.

I was fishing a run that had produced fish for me before and I had no reason not to think that there wasn't fish in there. I had made several casts through there and for whatever reason I didn't have a good cast and being a little bit irritated at my lack of prowess, I just ripped the fly around to get it straightened around in disgust. Then the rod was just about ripped out of my hand. Oh man! That was the hardest hit I ever had from a steelhead. I don't know what the deal was there. The only thing I could figure was that I stopped that fly right in the face of a fish and she hit it about 60 miles an hour. My rod just jolted and then she just screamed across the river. That was an interesting experience.

Clients

One of the biggest mistakes clients make is not setting the hook properly. Just simply not understanding how tough these fish are and thinking that simply raising the rod to set the hook is good enough. Simply feeling the pressure of those fish on the end of the line is not enough to set the hook. After they make the initial run and then stop and start to come back you really need to set the hook hard. It takes a sharp, hard hook-set; it's like trying to push a nail into a board or taking a hammer and hitting it.

What I tell people is to let the fish run and as long as you have good pressure the hook is not going to pop out. But that fish doesn't run from here back to Astoria. There's a time when that fish turns and comes back, at that time you drive that hook home and if you don't, my experience is that fish is gone within just a few minutes.

Other people if they have different experiences more power to them, but, boy. I do not find that the hook gets driven in just simply by the fish running away. That's one of the reasons why a lot of fish are lost at the last moment when they are close to shore. That's when the fish really gets to thrashing. That's a real critical point because your line has lost a lot of its elasticity. The fish can jerk the rod tip down, then come back against it quicker than your rod can respond. When you get some line out and get some stretch, it just adds to the flex of the tip of the rod.

Jeff Jarrett of Orofino, Idaho has been guiding steelhead fly-fishermen on the Clearwater River for the last 20 years.

Jeff Jarrett has been a licensed guide on the Clearwater for over 20 years and is one of the few guides who specialize in fly-fishing. Jeff was born in Lenore near the Clearwater River and probably knows the river as good as anyone that lives in the local area. Jeff guides out of Orofino and is usually booked with fly-fishermen from all over the world, from September through December. He has also spent a lot of time guiding in Alaska on the Good News River.

Jeff: I was born in Lenore. My folks had a cattle ranch down there for a long time at Bedrock Creek. I went to school in Lapwai and I've been pretty much of a river rat forever. When my folks got divorced I met this outfitter here in town named Leo Crane and I became his right-hand man. I was still in high school then, probably in '75 or '76. I was 15 years old. I could not guide legally until I was 18 in 1978.

Jeff Jarrett is one of the first fishermen who started fishing Articulated Leeches in several different colors.

Articulated Leech
(tied by Dave Clark)
Body: Crosscut rabbit, any color, use two hooks attached with 12-30 lb test monofilament

I've been fly-fishing since I was 9 or 10 at least 30 years. I started fly-fishing for steelhead in 1980. Up until that time I had been flinging gear and stuff. By 1981 I was fly-fishing only.

In those days, when I guided, it was from Orofino to Lenore for the most part. I went full-time guiding in 1984. I probably spent 100 days on the water and every year since then I spend more and more time on the water. In 1972 the State started dividing up the river into section where guides were allowed to work. In 1975 they divided it some more, and then about 1980 it changed again. The way it is set up in each river section, like Orofino to Lewiston is called Clearwater 3, and in that section there can be 10 powerboat outfitters which can have up to three boats per day fishing. I am licensed for two sections on the river, so I can have six boats in the water.

In order to be a guide in Idaho you have to work for an outfitter. Let's say on this river here, let's say you want to become an outfitter, you'd have to buy somebody out, and you'd have to buy their business. As an outfitter you can have as many guides as you want, but you can only have three boats on each section of water.

I fish a few basic patterns. I use a Wallie Waker, Bombers, Muddlers, Articulated Leeches. I use Articulated Leeches a lot once I go to sink-tips. In colder weather I use a sink-tip line. As soon as the water is forty-five degrees, I put the dry line away. The pattern really doesn't matter. You have to use something you think will work. It's all confidence. It's 100% confidence. When you tie that fly on, and you think maybe this will catch one and maybe this won't, you might as well get back in your rig and drive off 'cause you're not going to do any good on the water.

All of my fish are caught on the swing. Fling it and swing it. If you get too serious you're not going to catch them. It seems like when you're not paying attention and gawking around, Wham, fish on! There's no mystery to steelhead fishing. Get it in front of them and they'll take it. They'll let you know.

If I get a hit I just throw the same thing right back at them. Right at them again. If they don't take it within 2-3 casts then I'll riffle hitch a dry. Maybe throw a Bomber or a Waker out there. If they won't take that then I continue fishing on past them. Then in a half hour I'll come back after they've calmed down.

Generally when you have a hot fish, one that has whacked or chased the fly, calm down, catch your breath and go after them. They'll come back. When they feel aggressive they'll hit it again.

The most common mistake I see with clients is that they don't keep their line straight. They have too much slack out there. Most guys don't have a good feel for line management. They don't mend properly.

The first thing I ask a prospective client is how far can you cast? If they say 100 feet, I figure they can cast 50 feet maybe. Until I see you cast 100 feet, I don't believe it. Getting them to keep that fly and that line straight is a challenge. Most guys throw it out there, the fly ends up at the end of the line, all of a sudden you look out there and the tip of the fly line is here and the line is down there and the fly is traveling way too fast.

Most of the guys don't know how to mend. Guiding fly-fishermen is a no-brainer. Many of the guys will get frustrated. You have to be a psychologist, bartender, boat rower. Basically you need to just concentrate on having a good time. When you see them screwing up you just can't come out and say don't do that or don't do this. You have to use some psychology. You need to say something like, let me show you a trick, that's my favorite thing to say. I say, 'Here's a simple little trick.'

I tell people it's not about how many fish you catch with a guide, it's not about, 'Gee, I should have caught five fish today'. Hopefully I can teach you something or correct a bad habit. If everything works out, you're going to get into fish because the runs we're fishing and the spots we're fishing, I know there's fish there. I've been on this river forever.

This river can be full of boats and I have pocket water all day long I can stay away from everybody and still get into fish.

Last year it was awesome. Those big power boaters would go ripping up and down the river. You don't have to fish out in the middle of the river. The fish are right next to the bank. We caught a lot of fish right next to shore. These fish are not at all bashful. On this river, color seems to be a big thing. In the early season, you take any fly that is dark with a green butt and it will outfish every fly out there. Purple is good, purple is my rainy-day color. My basic color is all black.

If you go steelhead fishing with the attitude that you have to catch fish, you might as well stay home, because if you have to catch fish, you're not going to catch them. You're just beating your head against the wall. If you go out with the attitude that it's a great day, let's see what happens, you're going to catch every fish in the river.

People don't understand how important confidence is. It makes all the difference in the world. If I had one piece of advice for people that fish the Clearwater it would be, make sure the fly is in front of your line. I have seen so many times when a guy will throw a fly out there without mending and I have seen that fly take off and the guy doesn't know he has a fish on. I watched the end of their fly line go up and down and they don't realize they've had a take.

Bert Moffitt was a local fly-fisherman I knew. He passed away about three years ago. He was 85 years old. Bert used to fish with Lannie Waller. He started fly-fishing the Clearwater for steelhead in the late 50s. When I first met him he said, 'Sonny, I'll tell you something,' 'What's that?' I said.

Bert said, "I'm only going to tell you this one time, if you throw that fly out there and you throw your line up above it, you'll catch more fish." In other words, throw a mend in it.

I have a coronary when I see the trout fishermen that have to go steelhead fishing. He has too many bad habits to break. That's the guy if they don't have a fish on in five seconds they get upset. They are two totally different sports. The techniques are totally different.

People say that the fish are showing up sooner this year, but I haven't noticed any difference. There's always been some early fish that start showing up in June. What you are seeing is that there are more people fishing now and the word is getting out. They've always been here. We've always had a summer run that comes through here. They can be caught on small dry flies in the summer.

A lot of the fish in the Clearwater in the summer are lost. Many of them are Snake and Salmon river fish. There are a lot of fish that have already arrived at the dam. They've already taken steelhead in the hatchery. What will happen is that these early fish will stay here until we get a rain and that will change the chemistry of the river and pow they're gone. It's like someone turning on a light switch.

I hear people say that most of the B-runs are showing up later and later each year but frankly I haven't seen it. We get into big 40-inch fish every year up here by Orofino by early September. On the 15th of October, when catch-and-keep opens, you will catch steelhead that are extremely dark because they have been sitting in the river since June or July. I'm telling you, the biologists around here think they've got it down to a science and they really don't. I don't think they know all that much about steelhead.

The biggest fish I ever caught in the Clearwater was 29 1/2 pounds. When I first hooked it I thought I had foul-hooked something because it felt so different. It went up and down the river for a good 30 minutes. It wouldn't fit into my net when I got it in close. I ended up throwing rocks at him to chase him up onto the rocks so I could land him. I thought it had a good chance of being a State record. It was 45 1/2 inches long.

I think the size of the big wild fish has gone down some. They are a lot thinner than they used to be. When they used to show up they were girthy, not anymore. The length is there, but they are snakes. That's kind of sad, but I think that has to do with, see the big ones are traveling right now in August. They are here now.

They sit and sit for 2-3 months before they start to do something. From what I understand from what the biologists tell me, they lose a third of their body weight by the time they get here. That's a lot of weight.

Stories

Three years ago we had this fish; he was a big hatchery fish at a little spot we know of. When the water gets down, there's pretty good-sized rocks out there and there was this male that stayed there all winter. We called him Freddie, the Big Red Slim. He had a big red stripe down his side. We caught and released him five times that winter. He held in three feet of water all winter and if you knew where to look you could see him. He always came back to the same lie after he was released. We would come back a week later and there he would be. He was a decent fighter. Caught on a fly every time. He was 40 inches.

In his river, once it turns cold, the fish just stop. When the river is clear on a sunshiny day, you can float down the river and see most of those fish holding in the shallow water right next to shore. They are holding in the frog water. You can easily spook them if you immediately start wading without fishing short casts first.

I used to think that in the cold-water conditions that you had to put the fly right on top of them, but that doesn't always hold true.

I fooled around here one time and found one of Bob Wagoner's top-water flies one winter so I thought I would play with it. Darned if I didn't have two steelhead chase it and there was ice on the edge of the river. It was a waking fly in the winter time.

The only thing I know about these fish for sure is that they'll take a fly if it's presented right. As far as why they take it, what they see. Every time I think I've got it figured out I can't catch them. If I quit trying to figure it out so much and just go fishing I do a lot better.

I love Bombers a lot more than a Muddler. They really throw out a good wake. It's that turbulence that gets the fishes' attention. I want a V in the water like the Queen Mary out there. I want that thing making enough commotion that it gets their attention. You know those steelhead lay on the bottom, but their eyes are always looking up. Always looking up. If you can get them to see what's going on they'll go after it.

I use huge hooks, up to 2/0. I don't use small flies at all, bigger the better, I say. If you keep pressure on them, the hook won't turn loose. I use big articulated leeches. I tie the two hooks together using 65-pound-test braided line. They can take 30 minutes to tie, but they are a great fly. They are a real pain in the ass. The hooks are always sticking you in the fingers and hands.

About eight years ago I started fishing a two-handed rod and that's about all I've used since. I love them. You can fish water that you never could before. I use the single-handed rods out of the boat. The two-handed rods don't work well out of a boat. There's too much line.

Walking and wading, the Clearwater is ideal for two-handed rods. I mean you can cover 100 foot swings. The longer your fly is in the water, the more fish you are going to catch.

1990s

Dave Clark of Clarkston, Washington is an avid steelhead fly-fisherman and expert fly tier.

Dave Clark

Dave Clark has become a fixture on the Clearwater and Snake rivers for several years. How many times have you heard guys say that when they retire that they are going to spend their remaining days fishing? In many cases and for a variety of reasons these proclamations never come to pass. Dave Clark didn't make that mistake. When Dave retired in 1995 he looked around the Northwest for an area with a mild climate and a location where he could fly-fish for steelhead and other species several months of the year. He landed in Clarkston and has been fishing ever since. Dave fly-fishes for steelhead at least 60 days each year on the Clearwater and Snake rivers.

Dave: I lived in Spokane for several years and in 1980 a friend invited me to steelhead fish with him on the Columbia River near Pasco, Washington. The only stipulation he had was that we had to fly-fish. I borrowed an outfit from his friend for that first trip to the Columbia and succeeded in catching three fish on #8 Green Butt Skunks. After that I was hooked.

When I got back to Spokane I gave away my spinning outfits, built myself a steelhead rod and learned to tie steelhead flies. In 1992 I began fishing with a 13 foot Spey rod and now use that outfit exclusively. Most of my fishing on the Clearwater is in September. After that I fish the Snake River to avoid the crowds.

I generally don't fish past February 15. I think by that time the fish deserve a rest as they prepare to spawn.

I normally catch 80-120 steelhead each year and about 60% of those fish were caught before September had expired. I usually average 1-2 fish per trip, but it is not uncommon to go home without a hookup. However, the very next day I might catch more than two in the same water.

For the first five years I fished almost exclusively with Green Butt and Purple Butt Skunks. After purchasing Trey Comb's book I started tying and using a lot of the traditional patterns found in that publication, but now I find myself fishing about five main patterns in sizes ten to two. Including the two skunk patterns, I use the traditional Fall Favorite, Beats Me (local pattern) and a Doc Spratley. I don't always subscribe to the dark fly/dark day, bright day/bright fly theory. Many times at sundown I will put on a Fall Favorite and do very well.

Most of the water I fish on the Clearwater does not exceed six feet in depth, with the exception of the larger pools. The dominating characteristic of the Clearwater is its clarity and I think it compares with the famous Bulkley River in British Columbia in size and in clarity.

The Clearwater runs east and west which means the sun comes up in the fishes' eyes. From 11:00 to dark makes for better fishing when the sun is no longer in their eyes. However, in July and August I will start fishing at sunrise to avoid the hot temperatures that arrive by midday. I normally will fish one fly for 20-30 minutes in sizes 4-6. If it is a slow current I use a fly with Spey-type hackle and will use a smaller fly in the faster water. The larger hooks (greater than #2) are not necessarily an advantage in hooking and landing a fish. A big hook many times will embed itself in the bone and will gradually work its way loose. It is a lot better to hook fish in the side of the mouth through the skin. Nothing is tougher than a fish's skin and a smaller hook will not generally pull loose.

The last two years I've started fishing the early fall months with dry-fly patterns such as Bombers and Muddler Minnows. I use a 14 foot leader and many times the leader is the only portion of the line that is actually in the water. Two years ago on the Clearwater in August, just for the heck of it I put on a yellow-bodied Muddler Minnow and as the fly started to swing I was able to watch a shark-like dorsal fin cut through the water and follow it all the way to the end of the swing where I watched it come out of the water to engulf the fly. I was so transfixed that I didn't set the hook which was probably a good thing. The fish measured 37 inches and the whole experience

Lamplighter
(tied by Dave Clark)
Tag: silver tinsel
Body: Red with silver
rib
Hackle: Mix of yellow,
black, and red

Some of the largest steelhead caught by Dave Clark were on a Lamplighter pattern.

has encouraged me to use dry flies a lot more during the early season.

I've caught fish up to 38 inches on the Clearwater, but those fish are the exception. Both the Snake and the Clearwater rivers are good for drift boats or pontoons and allows a fisherman to fish water on the other side which is inaccessible to foot traffic. The biggest aggravation on the Snake River are the large tour boats that create large wakes as they zoom by. That is another reason why I like to fish the Snake early in the morning because you get about two good hours of fishing without being bothered by boat traffic.

I like a Spey rod, not because of its ability to make longer casts but for the ease of mending and line control and I like how they perform in windy conditions. Most of my fish are caught 20-30 feet from shore, but I've caught many fish, especially in the Snake, in water that a traditional rod cannot reach.

The Snake is a lot bigger river and a Spey rod is definitely an advantage, where one can hook fish with a 100 foot cast. The Snake runs north and south and the early morning fishing on the Snake is better than the Clearwater. One day, above Asotin, I released nine fish before 8:00 a.m. After having such a great morning I went home and ate breakfast and then returned to fish the same water in the late afternoon without touching even one fish.

On the Snake I like to look for small points of land and fish below the slow quiet water that forms around these areas. I've caught fish as large as 340-inches in the Snake.

Later on in the season when it gets colder I will occasionally use a weighted fly but I prefer to use a sink-tip line with an unweighted fly. In the faster water, I use flies with short hackles and stay away from material such as marabou. However in slow-water conditions or frog water, the marabou and soft-hackle patterns do very well because they have a lot of movement and pulsate slowly in the milder currents.

A favorite technique is to hold a loop of line in my left hand as the fly is floating in the current. After the fly has reached the end and the line is fully straightened out I release the loop so that the fly will move downstream a few feet. Many times this has enticed a strike. If that doesn't work I always makes two slow strips before retrieving the line. I have caught a lot of fish on that slow retrieve.

Many fly-fishermen retrieve their fly too soon. One way to know when the line should be retrieved is to put a large dry fly on and count how long it takes the fly to straighten out from the time the line begins to make the swing. You will be surprised at how long it will actually take for the line to completely straighten out. Sixty to seventy percent of the fish I catch hit the fly halfway through the swing. In the early season I don't set the hook when I feel a strike. I let the fish do what it wants without consciously setting the hook. This allows the hook to become imbedded in the side of the mouth where it will usually not pull out. In the cold winter months I will set the hook because the fish are not as active.

One day on the Clearwater I hooked a fish using a #2 Green Butt Skunk. I got a strike on the first drift so I switched to a #6 Green Butt Skunk. When the fish struck, it immediately ran at least 150 feet down river where it then veered towards the shore. When it jumped completely out of the water to shake the hook, it landed on the rocks near shore where the hook pulled loose. I watched it flail around in the rocks for a while until it was able to flop into the water and go free.

Terry Nab

Terry Nab is a local Lewiston resident and one of the area's better steelhead fly-fishermen.

Terry Nab has been a resident of the Lewiston Valley for twelve years and has developed a reputation as one of the better local fly-fishermen. Craig Lannigan considers Terry to be one of the top two or three local steelhead fly-fishermen, which is high praise coming from Craig.

Terry: Fishing has driven my whole life and if I'm not fishing I'm building rods, building reels, tying flies, reading about fishing, or planning a fishing trip. I don't remember how I got started fly-fishing but to my recollection I have been fishing my whole life. I moved to Lewiston in 1991 and I'm not sure exactly why I moved here because I didn't know anything about the area before I came.

I fish a lot with Craig Lannigan and we both fish a little different. Sometimes he does better and sometimes I do better. I try not to mend my line a lot. I use a Spey rod a lot and whenever I can I will try to do an overhand cast. I try to cast as straight a line as I can. What that does is a couple of things.

First of all, a lot of Spey casters do that upstream mend because their leader isn't straight. I catch a lot of fish on the first 5-10 feet of the drift. I tend to cast straight out from me and not down river like a lot of guys do. I think a lot of guys spook fish because when they mend they make the fly move and it can scare the fish. You want to watch the bag in your line. If the bag goes below the fly then the fly is going to start to whip and it's going too fast.

I've had very good luck with steelhead on skated flies. I have caught two fish on the Clearwater with a dry fly on an upstream dead drift, just like you were trout fishing, but that's uncommon. Conditions have to be just right.

If I fish a run and have a grab, sometimes I will use a comeback pattern. Generally I'll go to a sparser-tied dark fly. One pattern I like to use is called a Night Dancer that I really like. However, if I do get that first grab I will immediately put the same fly right over him again. I don't believe in resting the fish.

I'm more into traditional aspects of fly-fishing. I tend to tie traditional patterns. I haven't succumbed to using a lot of the new materials that are coming out. I like the traditional materials just fine. I get a lot more enjoyment out of catching fish on traditional stuff that looks good and they have great names.

Many small tributary streams feed the Clearwater River.

Terry Nab ties and fishes several different colors of Muddlers when he is dry-fly fishing for steelhead.

Green Muddler

(tied by Terry Nab)

Tail: Yellow hackle fibers
Body: Gold hurl
Wing: Orange and yellow dyed turkey quill
Head & Collar: Spun green deer hair

Sometimes I will riffle hitch my flies. If you want to really have some fun, riffle hitch a Muddler or a Bomber in the middle of the body. It really creates a wake and sometimes can entice terrific takes.

The first time I fished the Ronde I hooked seven steelhead, I didn't land all of them, I was only using a 6-weight rod with 6-pound-test leader. I didn't figure I was going to hook anything. You need to remember that before I came here I had caught over 2700 steelhead in Michigan.

The line control in my opinion is the most important aspect of steelhead fishing. You need to learn how to control the speed of the fly and it's not something that's easily explained. In my case I think it's simply a matter of experience and paying one's dues by doing a lot of fishing.

I don't care how good someone is or what pattern they are using if they can't control the speed of the fly they won't be as successful as they could be. That's why I don't believe in casting 100 foot casts. At those distances, it's a lot harder to control the line. If there's a lie out there that can't be covered by a shorter cast then I might try it. But I will cover the water and try to wade so that a shorter cast can be made.

You have to watch the bag in your line and learn how to handle it. I've been doing it for 30 years and after a while you develop a feel or touch for how to control the speed of the drift. If you are really interested in learning what the fly is doing in the water in relation to the line, then fish with a large riffled fly. That way you can watch the fly all the way and see what it is doing. If the fly is throwing a rooster tail every few seconds, it's going too fast. The wake created by the fly should be steady and consistent and not be throwing any water up in the air at all.

I've had 20-pound salmon chasing a hitched Muddler 30 feet across the river with their head and back completely out of the water and their mouth wide open coming for the fly. I've never seen that with steelhead. I've had steelhead that have followed the fly all the way to the end of the drift and take the fly with just a little dimple on the water, it looks like a trout, until it turns and you realize it's a large steelhead.

I was fishing the Clearwater one day and I had a 16-pound steelhead hit the fly very hard and take off full-speed down river. I had a little bag in the line by the reel and when I went to pinch the line off it almost cut me to the bone by my thumb.

John Toker

John Toker of Pullman, Washington with a Clearwater steelhead in 2000.

John Toker, all of 28 years old, is too young to be a top-notch steelhead fly-fisherman, but he is considered by some, including Craig Lannigan, to be one of the finest steelhead fly-fishermen in the region. He has a lot of experience catching steelhead in the Great Lakes region and was a licensed guide for Orvis for a couple of years. Since he moved to Pullman he has been mentored by many, including Jim Palmershein, Dave Engerbretson, Craig Lannigan, Al Burr, Jake Gulke, Gordie Olsen and Stan Hendrickson.

Dave Engerbretson said about Toker: "I never saw anyone come along so fast and learn so much so fast and within months knew the rivers as good as the locals. He just knew the rivers better, places of the rocks, everything. He learned faster than anyone I ever saw."

John: I ended up out here in July of '99. I didn't have a job or prospects for a job when I came out here. I was dating a girl, she came out for grad school and I came along. I wanted to fish steelhead.

I fished for two weeks before I started looking for a job. I started fishing the Clearwater by myself. The first day that I went down in the evening and didn't have a strike, didn't see anybody catch a fish. Next day I went down in the morning, by 9:30 a.m.

I caught my first Northwest steelhead and frankly it was a dog. I caught it on a Skunk.

It didn't do a whole lot, it was a 7-8-pound fish and I was like so this is what I read about. This was in August. That fish was a little anti-clamactic. I fished a while longer, about an hour and a half later I switched to a sink-tip line, it was bright and sunny and I was fishing some deeper water, dredging bottom. All of a sudden the line just went dead, the whole world exploded, my line was going down river and the fish was jumping past me in the other direction cartwheeling all over.

I went, 'OH! *This* is what we're talking about.' And it proceeded to break off. So I'm shaking, and it's just a great time. So that was it, Great. So I'm fishing through all day and trudging around the river and beating myself to death. I didn't eat lunch, I think I was dehydrated, everything else, but dammit I was fishing.

Right at last light, I had gone back to a floating line and I was swinging a fly on the tip of this island and I caught my third fish on my second day of fishing for Clearwater steelhead. That was a more classic take, a great fight and I landed it as the sun was going down.

I thought that was great, I think I could get used to doing this. Then I went on a two-week dry spell until Jim Palmershein took me. In the mean time I was just looking for people that knew how to fly-fish. So first I was introduced to Dave Engerbretson and I contacted him. He got me started: Where to go, what I needed to have, who I needed to know.

I tie my own flies. For steelhead fishing I like to sit down by the vise, relax and tie something that is aesthetically pleasing and effective. To me line control is crucial in steelhead fishing. That comes with practice and building lines.

I don't like to nymph with indicators. I like to fish the classic down-and-across technique. For me the "tug is the drug." The landing and the releasing of fish is secondary, it's the tug I'm after. With an indicator it's not so exciting.

I know there are places where that technique is very effective because you can't fish it down and across. I like the artistic part

Purple Spey

John Toker ties and fishes several original patterns on the Clearwater River, one of which he calls the Orange Prawn.

Orange Prawn
(tied by John Toker)

Tail: Crystal flash and orange hackle fibers
Body: Yellow sparkle material with green guinea fowl or similar feathers
Hackle: Orange palmered

of fly-fishing, but I also like to catch fish. Ultimately I think people should do whatever they want and others shouldn't take away from other people. If they are enjoying what they're doing more power to them.

The biggest fish I ever caught was on a bright sunny day. It couldn't have been any clearer. I'll fish well after dark sometimes and do well. I get some really explosive strikes in low-light conditions. A lot of guys like to fish that time as the sun is leaving the river in the evening.

I find that there are two types of strikes. One is a reactionary strike and the other is more of a follow. As far as choosing flies I find that there is something in most flies that at one time or another is going to stimulate a reaction of some sort. It's not like we are fishing a hatch or something along those lines where they are keying in on a particular insect.

They're probably keying in on some color or thing that we have no idea of. Sometimes the best that we can do is to pick a fly that at one time or another has invoked a reaction from a fish. You have to realize that we're not looking at catching a dozen fish; one or two fish and you go home happy.

So if you can invoke a reaction from one or two fish from all the fish that you've swung that fly by it's a good day. So to sit there switching back and forth and worry about which pattern and which color and what size, you'll drive yourself crazy and you're still not any further ahead than if you just used one or two patterns.

As far as comeback patterns, this last year I started switching to 2/0 and 3/0 flies on the comeback and had fish just slam them. I know guys who use two sizes larger on a comeback pattern and not go smaller how a lot of guys do. I don't know that it really matters; I think the key is that it's something different. Go big to

small or small to big, light to dark, whatever. I started out with follow-up flies that were smaller now it's a big fly. Sometimes I've followed a wet fly with a dry.

It's my first year steelheading on the Clearwater. I ran out of work one evening, I was so obsessed with getting down there and catching one of those fish. It was a beautiful day. I ran down there. The first two runs I wanted to fish had people in them. I was getting frustrated, almost angry. I was all upset and went to a different spot.

I had my Spey rod and started casting, I was doing okay with it, I had probably been fishing half an hour and had a strong take in shallow water. It fired off across the river, well into my backing and ran this way and that. It was a beautiful day, early in the evening and I finally got it up to shore. It was a beautiful 16-17-pound fish.

I just sat there and cradled it, looked at it, pulled the hook out of the corner of its mouth, kissed him on the head, I always do that. Held him there in the current, it had fought so hard that it was pretty tired. He finally gained enough strength to slide out of my hands, wished it a safe journey and watched it swim away in the current.

I sat there thinking about what a hurry I had been in and how angry I had got, that I had to settle for a third choice in fishing spots, and I had just had this wonderful experience with this wonderful amazing creature. As I watched it swim away, I picked up my rod, stuck the fly in the cork, put the rod on the ground and sat there on a rock and watched the sunset and thought about how lucky I was to be able to experience such an amazing fish, and that was it. I watched the moon come up and I didn't fish anymore that evening. I sat there for 30 minutes, thinking and watching the sunset.

Dan Callahan
Photo Gallery

Casting on the Grande Ronde River.

Grande Ronde River.

Grande Ronde River.

The Grande Ronde River not far from Boggan's Oasis.

Jack Hemingway on the Grande Ronde River with a hatchery steelhead we barbecued that night.

Carol Hemingway, Patrick Hemingway's wife, fishing the Grande Ronde River.

Where is he now? Jack Hemingway's dog Partridge on the Grande Ronde River.

Mike Lawson releasing a "B" steelhead on the Clearwater River.

Grande River near Troy, Oregon.

"I'll wait here." Fred Arbonna and his dog at Cherry Run on the Clearwater River.

Ames, Francis H. 1966. *Fishing the Oregon Country*. Caxton Printers, Caldwell, ID

Arnold, Bob. 1993. *Steelhead Water*. Frank Amato Publications. Portland, OR.

Barrett, Peter. 1970. "The Real Ted Trueblood." *Field & Stream*. December

Benbow, Mike. 2001. Grande Ronde River, WA Stepping Back in Time. *Northwest Fly-fishing*, Vol 3. No. 3

Bradner, Enos. 1950. *Northwest Angling*. A.S.Barnes and Company. New York, NY

Combs, Trey. 1977. *Steelhead Fly Fishing and Flies*. Frank Amato Publications, Portland, OR

Combs, Trey. 1991. *Steelhead Fly-fishing*. Lyons Press. New York, NY

Conley, Clare. 1965. "The Great Steelhead Hang-Up." *Field & Stream*.. April

Engerbretson, Dave. 1983. "Idaho Treasures." *Fly-fisherman* Vol 14 No 6, Harrisburg, PA

Engerbretson, Dave. 1986. *Tight Lines, Bright Water: Travels with a Fly-fisherman*. Solstice Press, Moscow, ID

Gerlach, Rex R. 1966. "Grande Ronde: New Steelhead Paradise." *Field & Stream* October

Gerlach, Rex R. 1967. "Boom in Steelhead." *Outdoor Life*. June

Helvie, Kent, H. 1994. *Steelhead Fly Tying Guide*. Frank Amato Publications, Portland, OR

Holm, Don. 1970. *The 101 Best Fishing Trips in Oregon*. Caxton Printers, Caldwell, ID

House, Gale W. 1995. *Steelhead Fly-fishing Journal*. "Recollections." Frank Amato Publications, Portland, OR

Jarrett, Robert D. and Harold E. Malde. 1987. "Paleodischarge of the late Pleistocene Bonneville Flood, Snake River, Idaho," computed from new evidence. *Geol. Soc. of Amer. Bulletin, V. 99*

Johnson, R. and J. Oatman. 2002 *TA'C Tito'oqan News*. Nez Perce Tribe. Dec., 2002

Landeen, Dan S. and Allen Pinkham. 1999. *Salmon and His People: Fish and Fishing in Nez Perce Culture*. Confluence Press, Lewiston, ID.

Lane and Lane Associates and D. Nash. 1981. "The Clearwater River Indian Fisheries and Lewiston Dam." Prepared for Bureau of Indian Affairs. Portland, Oregon: United States Department of the Interior

Lawrence, Ed. 2002. "Chasing Steelhead on Oregon's Grande Ronde River." *Fly Rod & Reel,* April

Leopold, A. 1993. *Round River*. Oxford University Press, New York, NY

Lindgren, Waldemar. 1898. "The mining district of the Idaho basin and the Boise Ridge, Idaho." U.S. Geol. Survey, 18th Ann. Rept. Pt. 3

Lupher, R.L. and Warren, W.C. 1942. "The Asotin Stage of the Snake River Canyon Near Lewiston, Idaho." *Journal of Geology,* v. 50

Marshall, Mel. 1973. *Steelhead*. Winchester Press, New York, New York

Meyer, Deke. 1992. *Advanced Fly-fishing for Steelhead: Flies and Techniques*. Frank Amato Publications, Portland, OR

Miller, Rick. 1967. "Lesson of the River." *The Creel*. Vol. 5, No. 1

Nelson, Norm Jr. and Richard A. Furniss. 1972. "River on Its Deathbed." *Outdoor Life,* April

Nelson, Norm Jr. and Richard A. Furniss. 1972. "Disaster on the Snake." *Outdoor Life,* May

Nowak, Cathy M. 2001. "Grande Ronde Subbasin Summary." Northwest Power Planning Council

Ormund, Clyde. 1969. "One for the Governor." *Outdoor Life*, March

Petersen, Keith C. 1995. *River of Life, Channel of Death: Fish and Dams on the Lower Snake*. Oregon State University Press, Corvallis, OR

Rockwell, Cleveland. 1903. "The First Columbia River Salmon Ever Caught With a Fly." *Pacific Monthly* Vol. X, No. 4

Roskelly, Fenton. November 1968. "Grande Ronde River Land Eyed for State Park." *Spokane Chronicle,* Spokane, WA

Roskelly, Fenton. February 1974. "Anglers Ideas on Ronde Management Asked." *Spokane Chronicle,* Spokane, WA

Roskelly, Fenton. July 1974. "Proposals Are Heard." *Spokane Chronicle,* Spokane. WA

Roskelly, Fenton. August 1974. "Ronde Fish Limits Set." *Spokane Chronicle,* Spokane. WA

Roskelly, Fenton. November 1980. "Steelhead returning to Grande Ronde?". *Spokane Chronicle,* Spokane, WA

Roskelly, Fenton. March 1984. "Outdated TV Show Rouses Fishermen." *Spokesman Review,* Spokane. WA

Roskelly, Fenton. March 1985. "Too Many Fishermen and Not Enough Fish." *Spokesman Review,* Spokane, WA

Roskelly, Fenton. June 1985. "Officials Puzzled by Reaction to Stream Trout Plan." *Spokesman Review,* Spokane, WA

Roskelly, Fenton. August 1986. "Clearwater River Issues Getting Muddy." *Spokesman Review,* Spokane, WA

Roskelly, Fenton. February 1990. "Steelhead Running for Record in NW". *Spokesman Review,* Spokane, WA

Roskelly, Fenton. October 1990. "Steelhead Counts Down, But Don't Be Discouraged." *Spokesman Review,* Spokane, WA

Roskelly, Fenton. December 1991. "Super Steelhead Run Smaller." *Spokesman Review,* Spokane, WA

Roskelly, Fenton. January 1992. "Steelhead Fishermen Loving It." *Spokesman Review,* Spokane, WA

Roskelly, Fenton. October 1992. "Big News for Steelhead Fishing in the Clearwater." *Spokesman Review,* Spokane, WA

Roskelly, Fenton. March 1993 "Don't Bypass Steelheading This Month." *Spokesman Review,* Spokan,WA

Spomer, Ron. 1987. "Forty Miles of Promise." *Sporting Classics,* Vol VI, Issue 4

Stacey H. Stovall. Editor. 2001. "Asotin Creek Subasin Summary." Northwest Power Planning Council

Trueblood, Ted. 1961. "I Found Steelhead Shangri-la." *True Magazine,* April

Trueblood, Ted. 1963. "Steelhead Fly-fishing." *Field & Stream*. October

Trueblood, Ted. 1967. "Crisis on the Columbia." *Field & Stream*. July

Tussing, Annette. 1971. "The Fight to Save the Snake." *Field & Stream*. Vol LXXVI No 6

Vallier, T.L. and P.R. Hooper. 1976. "Geologic Guide to Hells Canyon, Snake River." 72nd Annual Meeting Geological Soc. of America, Cordilleran Section, *Field Guide No. 5*

Vallier, Tracy. 1998. *Islands and Rapids: A Geologic Story of Hells Canyon*. Confluence Press, Lewiston, ID

Vincent, Jim. 1990. "A Steelheader's Journal." *Fly-fisherman*. Vol. 22 No. 1

Wheeler, Harry E, and Earl F. Cook. 1954. "Structural and Stratigraphic Significance of the Snake River Capture, Idaho-Oregon." *Journal of Geolog,y* Vol. 62 No. 6

Wethern, Robert. 1976. "Master Steelheader of the Ronde". *The Creel,* Vol 12 No 1

Index

A small tributary of the Clearwater River.

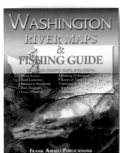

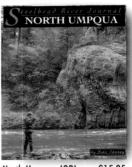
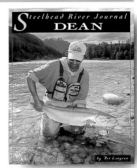

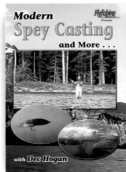

Fishing and Tying Books

Steelhead Fly Fishing in Nez Perce Country